Corporate Bankruptcy

Corporate Bankruptcy

Fundamental Principles and Processes

William J. Donoher

business**expert**
Press

Corporate Bankruptcy: Fundamental Principles and Processes
Copyright © Business Expert Press, 2012.

First published in 2012 by
Business Expert Press, LLC
222 East 46th Street, New York, NY 10017
www.businessexpertpress.com

ISBN-13: 978-1-60649-143-0 (paperback)

ISBN-13: 978-1-60649-144-7 (e-book)

DOI 10.4128/9781606491447

Business Expert Press Strategic Management collection

Collection ISSN: 2150-9611 (print)
Collection ISSN: 2150-9646 (electronic)

Cover design by Jonathan Pennell
Interior design by Exeter Premedia Services Private Ltd.,
Chennai, India

First edition: 2012

10 9 8 7 6 5 4 3 2 1

Printed in the United States of America.

Abstract

Corporate bankruptcy is becoming an increasingly important topic in today's turbulent environment. The bankruptcy decision can be a matter of life and death for the organization dealing with distress, but the impact of the phenomenon is magnified by the variety of business relationships in which companies typically are involved. Bankruptcy thus potentially affects customers, supply chain or network partners, managerial and non-managerial employees, landlords and many others in addition to the distressed organization. Understanding the bankruptcy process, therefore, can facilitate best-practice development and the protection of the organization's interests both before and after a bankruptcy petition. This book does not attempt to provide advice; each case is unique and should be addressed by competent legal counsel. Rather, this work is intended to provide an overview of the fundamental principles and processes of both Chapter 11 reorganizations and Chapter 7 liquidations, incorporating examples drawn from relevant legal decisions, research findings, and common experience to highlight the issues involved and provide a basis for discussion. In addition, the text covers the bankruptcy law implications of a number of special topic areas, including small business bankruptcies, governance issues, contractual agreements and obligations such as franchising and collective bargaining agreements, and newly emerging issues surrounding the use of derivatives.

Keywords

Bankruptcy, Chapter 11, Chapter 7, reorganization, liquidation, solvency, distress, creditors, priority, governance, contracts and collective bargaining, franchising, derivatives

Contents

Acknowledgments

The poet John Donne famously observed that no man is an island. At no time is this statement truer than when one embarks upon a project such as this. So many are involved in one capacity or another that it is impossible to enumerate each individually, even though their participation, involvement, and support are etched indelibly in my mind and will always be appreciated. I am grateful, first, to those who taught me or served as mentors in my professional and academic careers. Without their examples and knowledge, painstakingly (and sometimes painfully) passed on to me, I would not have been in position to write such a book. I hope my work reflects well on their efforts.

I am, of course, deeply indebted to those who directly participated in this endeavor. I would like to thank David Parker and everyone at Business Express Press for their assistance, support, and patience throughout the process. I could not have completed this work without you. I would also like to acknowledge and thank Al Warner and Bill Judge for stepping in with editorial advice and comments; their insights contributed to making this a better work.

And that brings me to a final acknowledgment: Mason Carpenter. Mason served as the original editor for this project, tragically passing away before its completion. He was always encouraging and believed in my efforts even when I wasn't that sure where I was going or whether I could get there. His loss is felt in the field, but more so in my work on this book. It is a great personal disappointment that I could not reward his support with a finished product, but I can say confidently that his support contributed to my ability to finish and produce what I hope will be a valuable, or at least useful, reference for students and the business community.

All of these, and indeed many more, made this work possible. Any errors or omissions are mine and not theirs. I hope you, as readers, appreciate and benefit from their input.

William J. Donoher
Springfield, Missouri

CHAPTER 1

Introduction and Overview

Bankruptcy is about relationships. We are not referring here to personal relationships, of course, although sometimes the personal relationships may intrude on bankruptcy proceedings—and in mostly unpleasant ways, it might be added. (Few better examples of this phenomenon exist than the experience of the Los Angeles Dodgers' recent bankruptcy, which was intertwined with the bitter divorce proceedings of the club's owners). Rather, bankruptcy is the story of the relationship of a debtor with its various creditors, and of the relationships between and among the creditors themselves. These relationships typically arise within a complex array of contract and practice, clarity and confusion, familiarity and surprise—all set within the context of varying state and federal laws, and all giving rise to expectations, rights, and remedies. How these relationships "work" within the context of a bankruptcy proceeding, and how they ultimately are resolved, is the topic of this book.

This text is intended to provide a practical, but comprehensive, look at the bankruptcy process under U.S. law.[1] Our coverage will begin with a review of the history and development of bankruptcy law in order to provide insight into the competing policy considerations that lie at the heart of bankruptcy law, and how today's Bankruptcy Code (the "Code") resolves the ensuing tensions of those policy debates. Discussion of the substance of bankruptcy will begin in the next chapter with the basic mechanics that apply equally to any type of filing, whether liquidation under the Code's Chapter 7 or reorganization under Chapter 11.[2] This will be followed in Chapter 3 of the text by a look at the definition and treatment of property interests and claims in bankruptcy. Chapter 4 begins with an overview of liquidation procedures, followed by consideration of the basic mechanics of reorganization, especially including the development and confirmation of the plan of reorganization. The final chapter of the text will look at a selection of specific, advanced topics of bankruptcy practice such as governance; small business bankruptcy; the implications of organizational structure and form, including franchise arrangements; and the treatment of derivative contracts.

This book attempts to consider and present not just the letter of the law, but also the strategic implications of the actions and decisions of debtors and creditors outside (and often prior to) bankruptcy and within the specific context of a proceeding. In furtherance of this process, text Chapters 2–4 highlight various "Battlegrounds," representing the critical decision points discussed in that chapter. Readers may choose to begin with these issues as a means of understanding the "forest" of the typical bankruptcy case before proceeding to the "trees" of some of the more technical topics. Indeed, if you find that you're becoming mired in the detail and complexity of the law, I highly recommend stepping back at least momentarily and reviewing the Battlegrounds to restore perspective. Figures 1.1 and 1.2 also help in this regard; each presents a schematic overview of major portions of the bankruptcy process that can help the reader focus on key issues and understand their relationship to one another and their place in the overall scheme.

As author, it is my hope that you take away from this work both a basic understanding of the law of bankruptcy and a sharpened sense of the legal consequences of specific developments faced either within your organization or by those with which you deal. Always remember, though, that each case is unique and may involve specific issues beyond the coverage of this book; expert advice and counsel, therefore, is critical, but this book can help you understand and identify basic issues. And issue recognition, even if one is uncertain of the specific resolution of a particular case, is often the first step in avoiding adverse consequences.

1.1 A Bankruptcy Tale

In order to get a feel for the bankruptcy process, let us begin with a look at an actual proceeding. Prior to its on-field success, culminating in World Series appearances in 2010 and 2011, the Texas Rangers baseball club's bankruptcy made headlines in mid-2010 and provided a rare, high-profile overview of reorganization in action. Although the bankruptcies of Lehman Brothers, General Motors, and Chrysler undeniably were

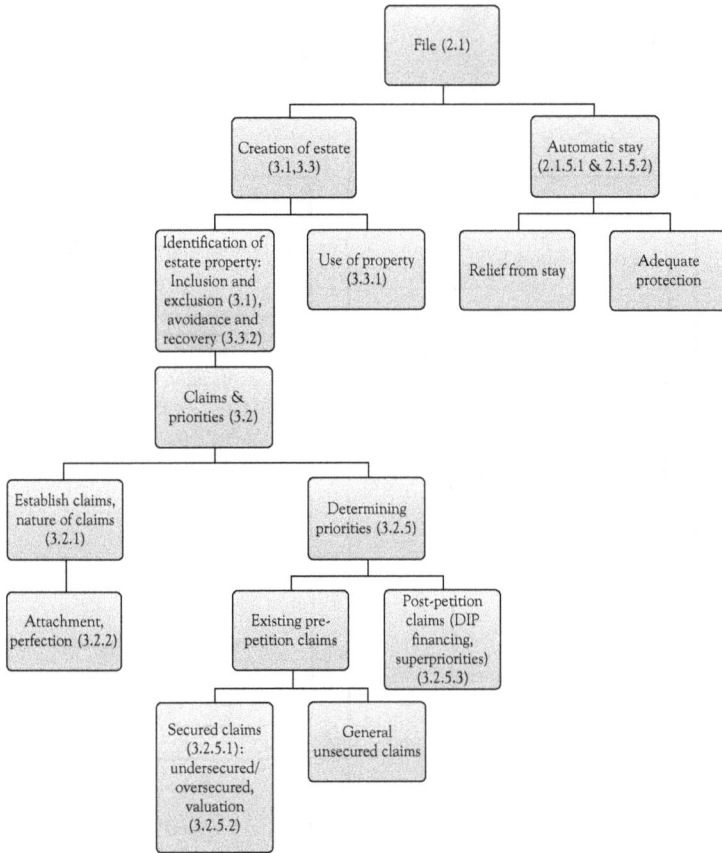

Figure 1.1. Overview of general Bankruptcy process. Applicable to all cases, whether liquidation or reorganization. See text, Chapters 2 and 3. Parentheticals refer to applicable text sections.

bigger and even more widely publicized, the details and circumstances of those cases made them somewhat unusual, as we will discuss later. And although every case is different in its own particulars, the Rangers' bankruptcy contains interesting illustrations of the typical parties involved in a bankruptcy proceeding, the complexities of their relationships with one another and with the debtor, and the general mechanics of reorganization under the Bankruptcy Code.

The story of the Rangers' decline into bankruptcy can be traced at least to 2005, when the organization began experiencing cash flow difficulties in the face of increasing debt and payroll obligations.[3] Financier Tom

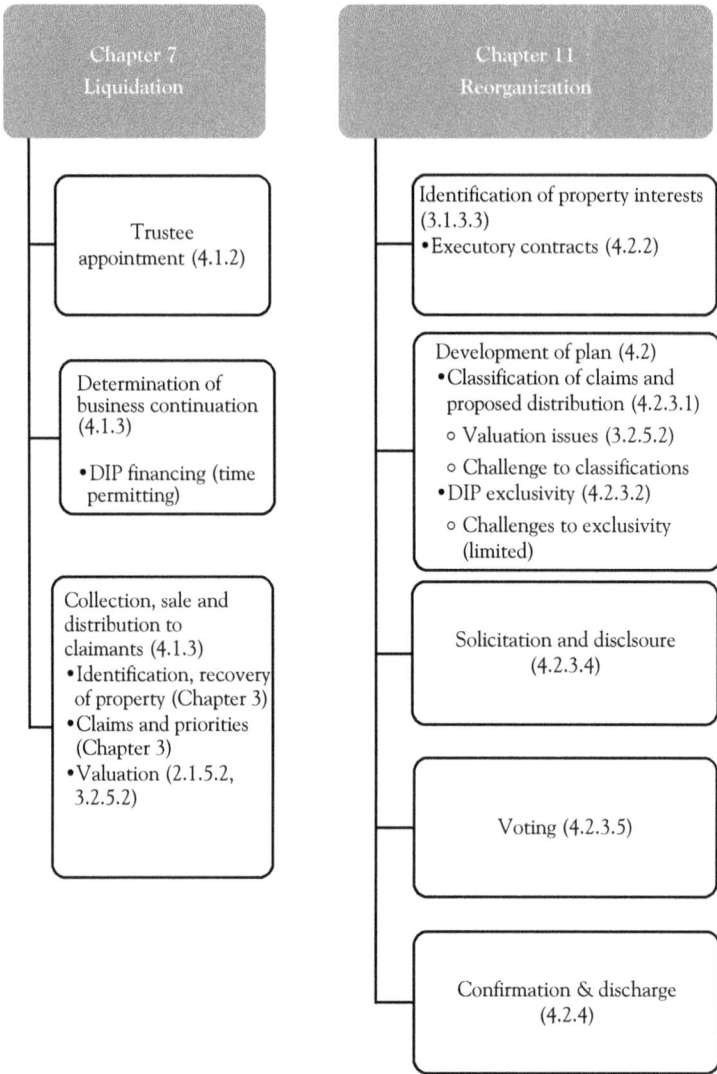

Figure 1.2. Chapter 7 and Chapter 11 Bankruptcy processes. Parentheticals refer to applicable text sections. Remember that motions to convert may be made at any point and in either type of case. See Section 2.1.2.

Hicks, co-founder of a private equity firm, purchased the club in 1998 through the Hicks Sports Group (HSG), which also owned the Dallas Stars hockey team and, later, the Liverpool English soccer club. After historic contracts with dubious economic returns, HSG was deeply indebted and arguably insolvent, struggling under a debt load of some $525 million, of which the Rangers became liable for $75 million through direct obligations or guarantees.[4] HSG defaulted on that indebtedness in April 2009, and in response Hicks announced plans to sell the Rangers in order to raise the capital necessary to repay the obligations.

By the end of that year, various partnership arrangements to buy the Rangers had coalesced around a group led by Nolan Ryan, the Hall of Fame pitcher who played for the Mets, Angels, Astros, and Rangers during a long and extraordinary career, and Chuck Greenberg, a prominent sports attorney. By January of 2010 an agreement was reached to sell the club to the Ryan–Greenberg group for around $525 million, including debt assumption. Major League Baseball (MLB), whose bylaws require league approval of prospective team owners, approved the ownership group represented by Ryan and Greenberg. Everything seemed to be in place for a smooth transition.

Unfortunately for the owners-to-be, the transaction did not encompass a simple transfer of an equity interest. There was the not insignificant matter of the disposition of the team's indebtedness and the rights of its creditors in the face of an existing default. In February 2010, the creditors notified the parties that the proposed sale would, in their opinion, realize insufficient proceeds to satisfy their claims, and they argued that MLB's acceptance of the Ryan–Greenberg bid, and apparent favoritism toward the prospective owners, violated banking laws in its failure to consider potential competing bids that would raise more cash.[5] With lawsuits pending from various parties, including lenders and former business partners of Hicks and/or HSG, the Rangers filed a "prepackaged" bankruptcy petition on May 24, 2010, including within their proposed plan the sale of the team to the Ryan–Greenberg group. Also part of the bankruptcy proceeding was the team's stadium lease and a parcel of land adjacent to the stadium.

This still did not settle matters. The lenders immediately objected to the proposal, and announced the availability of a then-unnamed bidder who would offer more for the club. The U.S. Trustee for the case filed a motion seeking to treat the petition as a traditional bankruptcy petition (rather than a prepackaged petition), which would require more formal procedures and voting under direct court supervision.[6] Bankruptcy judge

Michael Lynn ordered a revision of the plan to permit the lenders to pursue an alternate financing package. The planned conclusion of the bankruptcy case was postponed to July 22, but by the end of June, MLB was threatening to assume control of the club, while reports surfaced of yet another potential buyer. Meanwhile, another creditor sued on the stadium lease, claiming it had been fraudulently transferred from HSG to the Rangers.[7] This represented a significant complication in the proceedings, for without the stadium lease the team would have been worth substantially less.

Amid the procedural turmoil on the owners' side, the creditors' collective position began to get more complicated as well. On June 4, Alex Rodriguez, the star third baseman of the Yankees and a former Ranger, was named as a representative of the unsecured creditors' committee. Rodriguez, who signed a then-record $252 million contract with the Rangers in 2000, was still owed roughly $25 million in deferred compensation. As a group represented by the committee, the unsecured creditors took no immediate position on the pending sale of the team, but clearly they represented yet another voice at the table—and possibly another, and different, perspective that could result in a conflict of interest among the creditors themselves. Moreover, the committee representing the unsecured creditors was itself arguably a walking contradiction, encompassing not only player claims but also numerous small businesses that had outstanding claims against the team.

Ultimately, in order to satisfy the creditors and reach a supportable outcome, the bankruptcy judge ordered a sale at auction. The Ryan–Greenberg group was still in position with its offer to purchase the team, but a group led by Mark Cuban, owner of the Dallas Mavericks basketball club and presumed favorite of the creditors, emerged as a serious competitor. This event raised the ancillary issue of MLB's approval, since there was some speculation that Cuban might not receive the necessary support of existing franchise owners. The ability of MLB to enforce such restrictions against a bankruptcy judgment was in some doubt, adding yet another layer of complexity to the proceedings.[8]

After much additional procedural wrangling, the auction commenced on August 4, 2010 and lasted most of the night. Descriptions of the proceedings include accounts of high tension and a number of heated verbal exchanges as the parties added to and changed their bids in response to one another's proposals.[9] Much of the back and forth between the bidders concerned the structures of their offers and the valuation of the net realizable proceeds. Ultimately, the Ryan–Greenberg group walked away from the courtroom as owners of the Texas Rangers after entering a bid of $608 million, including debt assumption.[10] Creditors were to receive only $75 million from the team, representing the value of its guarantees of other parts of the HSG indebtedness, but were cleared to pursue HSG's other assets to satisfy the outstanding indebtedness.[11]

Obviously, this case is not typical of most business bankruptcies in specific terms—unless one owns a sports franchise. But, as noted in the opening, it does illustrate a number of general characteristics of bankruptcy practice. To begin, note the presence of two issues relating to the role played by creditors. First, it was the creditors, rather than the owners, who enjoyed the right of protection. Indeed, the resort to an auction was specifically intended to afford the greatest possible recovery to the creditors, without regard to the interests of any other party to the proceedings. Ownership was at best secondary throughout the adjudications, and in this particular the case mirrors the roles of creditors and shareholders encountered in the typical business reorganization. Herein lies an example of a key principle in bankruptcy procedure: Bankruptcy is designed to maximize creditor recovery, not to protect existing equity owners.

This point is further illustrated by the nature of the filing itself. Initially, the team filed what is known as a prepackaged plan, normally an arrangement in which the debtor negotiates the details of reorganization prior to filing and submits its reorganization plan concurrently with the bankruptcy petition.[12] With the foundation having been set in place, confirmation usually follows fairly quickly, hence the attractiveness of the device in cases in which the parties involved have no substantial disagreements or are able to pre-negotiate those disagreements. In this case, it appears that the team thought it would be able to secure confirmation on the basis of a plan that provided at least some creditor recovery and an improved ownership structure supported by MLB. But the creditors did not perceive this plan as the best possible outcome for them, and their contentions obviously prevailed. The prepackaged plan was set aside, an auction was ordered, and a final settlement was reached that provided maximum creditor recovery.

But even though creditors as a whole had the power to shape the nature of the proceedings, the second interesting issue raised by the Rangers' bankruptcy is the clear distinction between different groups of creditors. Although we often tend to think of bankruptcy proceedings as a battle between "creditors" and "owners/shareholders," in fact "creditors" come in many different flavors, having interacted with the debtor organization in many different ways—and sometimes involuntarily. Indeed, creditors and other claimants may have significantly different interests and opinions from one another concerning the preferred outcome of the case. The fact that they also may have different rights and powers under the Bankruptcy Code actually does little in most cases to minimize intercreditor conflict, and indeed often stimulates greater conflict as those without the status of others attempt to improve their standing or challenge outcomes that favor the preferred parties. Differences among creditors are indeed built into the process not only with respect to the nature of their claims but also with respect to representation: As we saw, creditors' committees were established in the Rangers' bankruptcy, a common approach in all but the smallest cases when the court is convinced that it would be unwieldy to deal with each creditor on an individual basis. The creation of these creditor "tribes" also can promote conflict between, and even within, creditor groupings. We will discuss this issue subsequently as we cover the mechanics of the reorganization process and the development of a plan that satisfies (most of) the claimants to the case.

The case also shows us the complications that exist when other parties, not formally creditors in the sense of lenders of capital under a formal agreement, assert their rights against the debtor organization, whether under contract or law. These parties, such as the players or those involved in the lease dispute, or, to use a more common example, tort claimants pursuing a product liability claim, are treated by the Bankruptcy Code as "creditors," but the specific nature of their relationships with the debtor organization and/or other parties may significantly complicate the case and alter the anticipated or desired outcome. And whether or not these parties possess the same rights as consensual creditors, such as lenders, their interests and claims must be accounted for and included within the final settlement of the case.

Also present here are the implications of the debtor's specific corporate structure. Notice that of the various HSG interests, only the Rangers were placed in bankruptcy. Although the Rangers were obligated on a significant portion of the indebtedness of the other parts of the HSG family, and in that sense intimately interconnected, it was not a requirement of the bankruptcy process for HSG to place all of its holdings and entities into bankruptcy. This does not mean that on the facts of a particular case the creditors could not force such a consolidation, perhaps by using the mechanism of involuntary bankruptcy or other legal maneuvers. But all such component parts of a greater corporate structure are likely to be independent corporations, thus giving the debtor "family" some latitude in deciding which parts are to be the subject of a bankruptcy proceeding. This decision, and the possible responses of creditors, represents one of the first potentially contentious areas in relatively complex bankruptcies.

Moreover, the lease dispute shows us what can happen in cases such as this. Recall that the argument centered on whether the team's stadium lease was improperly transferred from HSG to the Rangers, thereby cutting off HSG's creditors from a source of capital recovery. Although this scenario involved the transfer to the bankrupt debtor, transfers also may occur in the other direction, creating a problem for the creditors in the bankruptcy proceeding. Let us consider this for a moment: Suppose an organization has been struggling for some time, and it would not be surprising if it were to contemplate bankruptcy, even a full liquidation, at some point in the future. Indeed, perhaps decisions have already been made to do so, but there are important or significant assets that seem more valuable to the debtor than to any prospective creditor. Let us further suppose that other enterprises in which the organization has an interest (or perhaps simply other divisions of the same company) may have use for these assets. One obvious solution might entail the transfer of those assets to the other enterprises or divisions in order to preserve their value and improve the prospects of the other businesses. Under the Bankruptcy Code, this kind of arrangement likely would be voidable as a preferential transfer. Different tests apply to different kinds of transfers, as we will see later, but the intent is to preserve capital value *for the benefit of all creditors* and avoid the problem of hidden assets or "sweetheart" deals that favor only certain creditors.

Preferential transfers such as that just described may be voidable as unjust enrichment of a favored claimant, but the question of duty is even broader and may well predate the bankruptcy process itself. Consider again the Rangers' managerial history and decision-making. In whose interest did the club act when it entered into its various financial arrangements with players, partners, and financiers? Clearly, these decisions ultimately were responsible for the club's financial demise and descent into bankruptcy. Yet, in different circumstances, some or all might have worked. At what point, though, should club management have considered that, in the totality of present circumstances, an additional obligation or decision might not benefit existing creditors? Under ordinary circumstances, of course, the law presumes the existence of, and indeed imposes upon the corporation, the duty to represent and protect shareholder interests. But what do we do about the corporation heading in the wrong financial direction? The fundamental conflict between creditor and shareholder interests and representation rises to a new level when financial distress is at issue, but there is some case law suggesting that managerial duties must shift in favor of creditors when the firm is in the "zone of insolvency."[13] Precisely what this may mean in practice is yet another matter for case-specific investigation.

Finally, the Rangers' bankruptcy illustrates a fundamental issue at the heart of bankruptcy practice and process, and thus of this text: Bankruptcy, at least in the sense of a reorganization under Chapter 11, is not a deterministic process in which debts and obligations are toted up, matched against claim priorities, and allocated to all in proportion to their interests. Rather, reorganization is a negotiated process, one that requires accommodation of various and often competing interests, *largely because its purpose is to rehabilitate the debtor*. Although the Bankruptcy Code's greatest virtue is its rationalization and structuring of the process through an explicit system of rules, the actual application of that system to the particulars of a given case allows great latitude in the eventual outcome. Some may view this as a weakness, and perhaps in some cases it is. But, for the most part, the process is designed as a negotiation to produce an outcome that maximizes the interests of the greatest number of participants, including the debtor itself—an outcome similar to what mathematicians refer to as Pareto optimality. It is also important to note at this juncture that bankruptcy is not formally limited to cases of insolvency, extreme or otherwise. We will return to this issue later, but again bearing in mind the rehabilitative orientation of the Code, most parties' interests will be maximized when some core of the organization can be saved and rehabilitated, not when distress has reached such an extent that the firm may or may not be a going concern and a filing of reorganization is, in effect, nothing but a prelude to a liquidation.[14]

By this point in the discussion the complexity of the common bankruptcy should be apparent. But note the policy concerns implicated by the preceding paragraph, suggesting the ultimate purpose or intent underlying the structure of bankruptcy law. Indeed, as suggested early in this discussion, there are competing policy considerations that must be balanced in crafting a bankruptcy system. The story of those competing considerations and how and why the law developed as it did is the subject of the following section.

1.2 The History of Bankruptcy

1.2.1 Ancient and Early Modern Practice

Bankruptcy as we know it today builds upon surprisingly ancient precedents. According to Blackstone in his famous *Commentaries*, the word itself seems to derive from the terms in Latin or Romance derivative languages meaning "table" or "counter," on the one hand, signifying the tradesman's table, and either "road" (from the French *route*) or (from the Latin *ruptus*) "broken," on the other. Thus, the root meaning of the word seems to be "broken counter," conceptually signifying that an insolvent tradesman's shop or counter was broken or taken elsewhere (in keeping with the "road" reference from the French).[15] The historical development of bankruptcy, in both practice and legal foundations, is important not only as a matter of interest (or as grist for trivia to enliven social functions), but also for what it tells us about the policy of bankruptcy law. In short, what should society seek to accomplish in enacting any form of bankruptcy law? As we will see, there are two predominant themes that transfuse bankruptcy throughout history.

The fundamental concept of debt forgiveness can be found in Biblical texts of both the Old and New Testament eras. We also see the foundations of the modern concepts of priority, based in part on security interests, exemptions, and several other (mainly personal) bankruptcy procedures. But a parallel treatment, that of punishment for outstanding and unpaid debts, which Dickens so memorably described, seems to have originated in ancient Greece, where unpaid debts led to the enslavement of the debtor, his family, and his servants. Both concepts were joined in the Code of Hammurabi, the king of Babylon, *circa* 1780 BC, which provided for imprisonment, but which also contemplated a form of debt relief in the voluntary, but time-limited, enslavement of the debtor in satisfaction of the debt.[16]

Perhaps not surprisingly, the early Romans viewed the non-payment of debts with limited tolerance, and tended to permit the creditor to exact a portion of flesh in compensation—often literally. Later practice in the Roman Empire foreshadowed the modern concepts of attachment and execution by permitting the creditor to seek legal sanction for the seizure of the debtor's property. Following appropriate notice, the magistrate would summon the creditors and supervise the liquidation of the debtor's estate, but without discharging the debtor from responsibility. The practice thus permitted subsequent actions for collection of any deficiency against the debtor, including arrest. The emperor Augustus later amended the procedure to permit voluntary forfeiture by the debtor, again without full satisfaction of the debt, but subject to judicial protection of basic necessities (today's practice of exemption) and immunity from arrest.

Thus, for the most part the ancients clearly intended "bankruptcy" law to favor the creditor and to provide a means of recovery on the original obligation, whether in full or in kind. These practices were also incorporated into the comparatively more recent laws of England, from which U.S. laws are derived. Debt practice had begun in the 13th century following the institution of the first commercial relationships between the great estate lords and their bailiffs, but became more prevalent as commerce, and especially reliance upon debt contracts, broadened and deepened during the Middle Ages. More systematized practice was initiated by what is considered the first modern statute on bankruptcy, passed in 1542 during the reign of King Henry VIII and entitled "An Act Against

Such Persons as Do Make Bankrupt." Substantively, the law provided for an involuntary bankruptcy process, initiated by the creditor against the debtor and under which all of the debtor's property could be attached and liquidated, and the debtor himself imprisoned. There was no discharge from debt under the law, so the debtor remained liable for full payment of the underlying obligation in the (typical) event his property was insufficient to satisfy the debt. The 1542 Act was modified in 1570 by strengthening protection against fraudulent transfers (providing entitlement to double damages in the event of such transfers) and providing for a continuing right of attachment against after-acquired property or earnings.

Interestingly, most subsequent revisions and amendments in ensuing decades were aimed at forestalling or providing remedies against fraud and fraudulent transfers. Physical punishments were common, up to and including the death penalty ("without benefit of clergy") provided for in the Act of 1705. But the 1705 Act did begin the process of institutionalizing debtor protections such as full discharge. The discharge was not automatic, and had to be issued upon a finding by the presiding commissioners that the debtor had complied with the Act, evidenced by a "certificate of conformity," but a discharged debtor also could personally receive up to 5% of the value of the estate actually recovered by bankruptcy process (the allowance).

In 1732 British bankruptcy laws were formally revised and more extensively codified. The concepts of the discharge (as well as the death penalty for fraud) and allowance were retained but procedures were delineated for the first time. Although still pro-creditor in its orientation, the contemplation of debtor remedies and protections was an important accretion. More importantly, this was the law in effect at the time of the American Revolution and the drafting of the Constitution, and which therefore provided the foundation for the development of American bankruptcy jurisprudence.

Throughout this historical sketch, it is important to note the implicit tension between debtor and creditor interests. Obvious as that may seem in the context of an adversarial relationship in which one party's rights to payment conflict with the other party's ability to pay and rights to (perhaps) some form of protection, the precise balance between these interests may take any number of forms, as the illustrations discussed above suggest. Indeed, whether viewed from the perspective of reason, justice, or morality, sound arguments can be advanced for a law that tilts toward either side of the dichotomy. But a trend also should be observed: Early laws were exclusively pro-creditor, often authorizing harsh treatment of defaulting debtors, while subsequent enactments began to expand the range of protection afforded the debtor (absent affirmative wrongdoing on the debtor's part). The tension between the two sets of competing interests remains in today's law, including under the American Bankruptcy Code, which has tended to err on the side of the debtor for reasons of public policy. With this in mind, we turn now to consideration of the development of American law and today's Bankruptcy Code.

1.2.2 Development of American Bankruptcy Law

The United States Constitution provides the basis for a federal bankruptcy regime. In Article I, Section 8 Congress is authorized to "establish an uniform [*sic*] Rule of Naturalization, and uniform Laws on the subject of Bankruptcies throughout the United States." No other Constitutional provisions discuss or define bankruptcy, and there was much early debate concerning the distinction between bankruptcy and insolvency, and ultimately about the purpose or nature of a bankruptcy act. Federalist 42, written by James Madison, suggests that the founders contemplated bankruptcy laws as a necessary counterpart to normal commercial regulation under the Commerce Clause, and the nation's early economic history validates the systemic importance of an orderly reconciliation of financial distress.[17]

Despite its inclusion in the Constitution, no federal bankruptcy law was passed during the 1790s, when economic disruptions in both 1792 and 1797 led to the imprisonment of numerous debtors. Given the absence of a uniform federal regime during this period, state insolvency codes (note again the distinction between insolvency and bankruptcy) prevailed. This development actually was important beyond mere historical interest, for today's Code is built upon a foundation of state law that determines the nature of rights and entitlements of each party to the proceedings. Broadly speaking, the Code provides a framework and process for the orderly settlement and reconciliation of these pre-existing rights.

Thus, the bankruptcy process has both state and federal components, and the federal law often is viewed as an overlay of state law entitlements.

In the first century after the adoption of the Constitution, Congress enacted a number of different bankruptcy laws (passed in 1800, 1841, and 1867), none of which proved enduring.[18] Many reasons for this existed, not the least a nagging lack of consensus echoing the Constitutional debate between those advocating states' rights or sectional interests and those favoring a stronger national government. The first federal bankruptcy law, adopted in 1800, built upon pre-existing English jurisprudence, in part because of the view, then prevalent, that the Constitution imported the common law of England except as specified. Thus, the 1800 Act offered a primarily creditor-oriented framework in which only involuntary (creditor-initiated) petitions were allowed, and then only for merchants.[19] But the 1800 Act also introduced a limited discharge, albeit only with the approval of the presiding commissioners and the creditors.

The crisis precipitated by the 1837 panic led to reforms that were introduced in the 1841 Act. Critically, this law provided for the first voluntary petition in bankruptcy. The class of debtors, previously limited to merchants, also was expanded to include any and all who owed a debt. Involuntary procedures were retained, but limited to merchants, as under the 1800 Act. The distinction was the subject of fierce constitutional debate, between those who sought to limit the law to its boundaries at the time of the Constitution's adoption (principally John Calhoun, of nullification fame), and those (such as Daniel Webster, the primary sponsor) who sought greater equity. (Civil War aficionados should be interested in this juxtaposition of parties and ideologies.) Finally, the 1841 Act introduced limitations on preferential treatment of creditors by debtors, a precursor of today's practice. Despite these advances, the 1841 Act was repealed the following year, as creditors stormed Congress complaining about the law's laxity and favoritism of debtors, which had, in their view, resulted in a flood of bankruptcy petitions.[20]

The panic of 1857 and the Civil War resulted in a new interest in a federal system of bankruptcy law. Following repeal of the 1841 Act, state laws had proliferated, leading to a series of conflicts and "incomplete" discharges in which non-resident debts could not be resolved. This circumstance, as well as, it must be admitted, the desire of Northern creditors to more easily collect on debts owed by Southern debtors, led to passage of the 1867 Act. But the Act was something of a compromise between debtor and creditor interests, incorporating generally debtor-favorable state exemptions (property of the debtor deemed necessary to existence and thereby automatically protected) and providing for discharge upon payment of a 50% dividend on the existing debt. Tilting in favor of creditors, though, were provisions setting forth the grounds for denying discharge, which were so numerous that relatively few discharges were granted under the new law. In another jurisprudential first, though, the precursor to today's plan of reorganization was introduced.

What we see, then, in the nation's first century of bankruptcy practice is a gradual evolution toward a system of debtor protection, despite a series of fits and starts and seesaw-like exchanges between creditor and debtor interests. It was left for the Bankruptcy Act of 1898 to create the nation's first enduring framework of bankruptcy procedure, one that more clearly laid the foundations of bankruptcy practice observed today. The 1898 Act retained the voluntary petition for non-merchant (and non-corporate) debtors. At this time in the nation's economic development, the corporate form was being rapidly adopted for the first time, and the view was that its limitation of liability for individuals was sufficient protection. But in recognition also of the growth of the nation's "credit economy,"[21] the 1898 Act broadened the availability of discharge, principally by significantly reducing the number of available grounds for denial existing under previous laws, and by limiting creditor and even court input into the discharge process. Given the existence of these statutory grounds for denial, courts were only to determine whether the facts of the case fell within the stated parameters. Previously, courts played a more judgmental role and, of course, creditors were able to more easily contest the debtor's suitability for discharge. In effect, the 1898 Act created a presumption in favor of discharge, the first such in U.S. jurisprudential history. As Tabb notes,[22] this represented a significant departure from English law, where at the time reform efforts had removed the authority to grant a discharge from creditors but had only vested it in the court itself. But again, in a reaction to the supposed largess provided by the new Act, amendments in 1903 added new grounds for denial of the discharge.

Apart from the specification of grounds for denial, the 1898 Act also provided for certain debts that were to be excluded from the discharge, including taxes, fraudulently obtained credit, and fiduciary misconduct. The 1903 amendments also changed these provisions, adding, for example, alimony and maintenance payments. This general approach to exempted debts was continued in today's Code.

If we return to the original description of the 1898 Act, though, it will become apparent that one key provision was lacking: Corporate bankruptcy, or more specifically, corporate reorganization. Corporate debtors could liquidate, or more often, given the focus of the laws and politics of the day on the travails of the railroads, avail themselves of receivership actions. Absent was a uniform national law on the subject, and with debate still raging about the proper balance to be struck under the nation's federalist principles, state receivership and foreclosure laws were used to create judicially constructed "equity receiverships" under which businesses effectively could be reorganized.[23] The Chandler Act of 1938 responded to this situation and the gap in the 1898 Act's coverage by adding reorganization provisions (Chapter X for public companies and Chapter XI for private ones) to the 1898 Act and strengthening the bankruptcy referee's role to facilitate the reorganization process. Chapter X effectively shut down the receivership practice, once the province of elite firms servicing large and prominent corporate clients. (Recall that the New Deal was then in full flower.) But Chapter X also provided for mandatory managerial replacement by a bankruptcy trustee, thus creating a significant disincentive for companies to take advantage of the new law. Nevertheless, the Chandler Act, and its new reorganization provisions, marked the initial step on the road to a uniform system of national reorganization practice.

In reviewing the general patterns of the nation's bankruptcy laws, then, we observe once more the traditional tension between creditor interests and debtor protection that animated the development of bankruptcy law throughout history. But we also observe a trend favoring discharge and debt forgiveness, rather than the more punitive, creditor-oriented approaches of the past. Certainly there were many instances of creditor reaction that led to subsequent tightening in the law, but in general we see increasing interest in debtor protection. Whether this is good or bad public policy is not the purpose of this book to investigate or advocate, but it is the general purpose of the law, and indeed has been the underlying theory of the law's development, to facilitate debtor rehabilitation. On this viewpoint, the underlying assumption is that society is better served by permitting debtors, particularly corporate debtors, to reorganize and attempt a fresh start, unencumbered by previous obligations (at least in their original form). There is an economic argument to be made as well in favor of debt relief, and specifically corporate reorganization, to the extent that reorganization preserves net economic value. In theory, as long as a company is capable of generating value as a going concern, it makes sense to permit its continuation in business through reorganization. Note that this places the burden on the lender initially to screen its prospective borrowers more closely, and from an economic perspective may result in higher interest rates to compensate for the greater risk that the creditor assumes under such a regime. Such is the balance that society, through the laws enacted by Congress, has struck. We turn now to an overview of the adoption of the Bankruptcy Code and of its structural components.

1.3 The Bankruptcy Code of 1978

1.3.1 Genesis and Overview

For 40 years after the passage of the Chandler Act, which, we recall, was the vehicle by which corporate reorganizations were introduced into bankruptcy law, bankruptcy practice remained something of a backwater. Chapter X did not open the door to uniform reorganization, if only because of the disincentive created by its mandatory managerial displacement system. But there was an anomaly in the law. Chapter XI, which was intended for private corporations, commonly perceived to be the intended destination for small, family firms, did not by its terms exclude public companies otherwise subject to Chapter X from filing under its coverage. And there was one other significant difference between the two chapters: Chapter XI did not contain the mandatory displacement provision. Thus, many public companies attempted to use Chapter XI despite the law's intended use for private firms. The Securities and Exchange Commission (SEC), which had been given significant administrative responsibility for the law's oversight, challenged many of these filings, and specific terms of the prospective reorganization often were negotiated on a case-by-case basis.[24] The result was a sometimes conflicting series of legal standards and applications and a general hodge-podge approach to reorganization law that further reduced its appeal. Ironically, it was the rapid acceleration in the number of *personal* bankruptcy filings in the 1960s that ultimately led to the studies and commission reports that culminated in the Bankruptcy Reform Act of 1978.

For our purposes, the significance of the 1978 Act, which we have and will continue to refer to as the Code, lies in its structural approach to corporate bankruptcy. Several important changes enacted in the Code deserve mention at this juncture. First, the combination of Chapters X and XI into a single Chapter 11 had the effect of eliminating the 1898 Act's *de facto* distinction between large and small business bankruptcies.[25] Under the Code, any corporate debtor may avail itself of the protection of Chapter 11, or, in the alternative, directly seek to liquidate under Chapter 7.[26] The Code retained the involuntary petition provision found in prior laws, but in practice almost all filings are voluntary. Another significant change from the 1898 Act concerns the displacement of incumbent management, which, it will be recalled, made such changes mandatory upon filing. Now, under the Code, reorganizing debtors may retain their managerial team, and displacement by a trustee occurs only upon petition to the court under specific circumstances. This so-called debtor-in-possession rule removes the disincentive to filing that had existed under the 1898 Act. The theory for this change was that, if the goal of reorganization is the sustenance and continuation of the business as a going concern capable of creating economic value, then managers were the obvious choice to maintain operational control. As we will discuss later, the court significantly controls decision-making, since complete managerial autonomy would likely result in at least some wasteful expenditures that would deplete the value of the assets available to satisfy creditors' claims. But incumbent management, and not a trustee or receiver, is given at least the initial opportunity to settle the company's debts.

The Code also generalizes creditor interests, in the sense that individual creditors typically do not negotiate with the debtor organization; rather, as we saw in the opening vignette discussing the Texas Rangers' bankruptcy, committees usually are formed and appointed by the

U.S. Trustee. These committees enjoy specific rights, privileges, and powers, but also come with practical limitations, commonly including things such as unwieldy size, communication difficulties, and, most importantly, potential intercreditor conflict with regard to priorities and voting. These results follow from the procedural structure of the Code, which, unlike many of the previous bankruptcy laws that had relied more on creditor initiative and agreement, places initial responsibility for promulgation of the reorganization plan on the debtor (and remember, per the previous discussion, this means incumbent management). While each class must vote to approve the plan, not all creditors within a class need do so, as we will see later in this book. Provisions for overcoming creditor objections and even holdouts also are included, so that ultimately, while creditors do indeed determine the success of the reorganization and have substantial input into the debtor's affairs, the reorganization is intended by the Code to reflect more of a balance between the debtor company (again, usually management) and the creditors than was true under prior laws.[27] Note here that the usual concern of corporate governance raises its head in implicit form: Equity interests receive only cursory attention and have at best limited rights, yet it is the management team that is given the right to initiate the plan of reorganization—for the benefit of the creditors.

In sum, by replacing the existing (and substantially limited) regime of bankruptcy law with specific rules and procedures, and by giving specialized courts greater authority over the proceedings brought before them, the Code systematized bankruptcy practice. But a related outcome of the Code's structural approach has been the development of a formal bankruptcy bar, including both judges and practicing lawyers who specialize in the field. This trend had its origin under previous law, or at least under the disparity that existed between receivership practice and bankruptcy practice, but given the growth of formal structures and the prevalence of bankruptcy law in today's business and legal practice, the role of the bar is more pronounced. And given the formalization of practice and procedure, there is also a concomitant development of a culture within the bar that has been documented and discussed in the legal literature.[28] This may be good or bad, but it is important for all to understand its significance: Outcomes under a particular case may well depend upon standards of practice and understandings between counsel and judges built up over time. As in many areas of the law, what the law means may, in other words, depend upon who is advocating and who is adjudicating and what their respective, or joint, interpretations of a particular issue may be. This is not to suggest or allege corruption; rather, it is to acknowledge the practical implications of existing legal practice. Many issues are, of course, cut and dried under the express statutory framework offered by the Code, but others may involve questions that are of considerably grayer provenance where understanding the nuances of bankruptcy practice is important to evaluating one's subsequent decisions.

It is also worthy of mention here that the Code has been amended a number of times through the years, most recently in the 2005 Bankruptcy Abuse Prevention and Consumer Protection Act (BAPCPA). Recall in our discussion of bankruptcy history the number of times laws have swung between creditor and debtor interests, sometimes favoring one (usually creditors) exclusively or altering the balance between them in metronomic fashion. The BAPCPA generally dealt with individual cases and made it relatively more difficult for individual debtors to obtain full relief. This book will not be concerned with individual bankruptcy and thus will not elaborate further on these changes.[29] But in a related amendment, the distinction between small and large business bankruptcies was reintroduced (recall the 1898 Act's Chapter X and Chapter XI), ostensibly on the theory that individual abuses were to be curbed in either their human or corporate forms. There are now new rules governing small entities with no more than $2,190,000 in debt (the amount is to be adjusted periodically; this is the most recently promulgated figure, in effect from April 1, 2007). Note here that the test is debt-based, rather than asset-based. There are obvious incentives under this provision depending upon which method a debtor otherwise subject to the small business rules might prefer. In most cases, one would suspect a preference for the regular Chapter 11 rules, but note the possibility of "adjusting" one's asset structure in accordance with bankruptcy planning.[30]

The new rules pertaining to small business thus are problematic. While not requiring completely separate adjudication, as did the old Chapter XI, the BAPCPA imposes stricter filing and reporting deadlines on these entities than on their larger compatriots. As Professor Elizabeth Warren has pointed out, there is no evidence and little theory to justify the distinction and disparate treatment, but the structure of the advisory and drafting committees, which in general lacked small business representation, may have contributed to this outcome.[31] Indeed, the new rules seem to turn longstanding concern for the applicability of bankruptcy law to small debtors on its head: Previous work by Professor Lynn LoPucki documented extensive delays in reorganization cases attributable to the structure of the Code, which he argued were injurious to all but the largest debtors.[32] Therefore, a better set of reforms would have streamlined the procedure for small debtors; instead, we seem to have complicated matters. Time will tell whether these amendments improve the situation or simply add to the costs borne by small businesses.

1.3.2 The Structure of the Code

The Bankruptcy Code is divided into several chapters, each of which deals with specific proceedings, and all of which can be found in Title 11 of the United States Code (the body of statutory law passed by Congress). Related provisions can be found in Titles 18 (Crimes and Criminal Procedure), 26 (the Internal Revenue Code), and 28 (Judiciary and Judicial Procedure). There is also an accompanying body of procedural rules, codified as the Federal Rules of Bankruptcy Procedure. We will be concerned with the latter only tangentially, to the extent the rules elaborate on statutory language.

The subdivisions of Title 11 can be summarized as follows:

- Chapter 1—General provisions, including definitions, rules of construction, and clarification of who may be a debtor under the various statutory frameworks.
- Chapter 3—Case administration, covering issues such as commencement of a case; duties and eligibility of officers, such as trustees; notice requirements; creditor meetings; and general administrative powers, including the automatic stay; and limitations on the use, sale, or lease of property.
- Chapter 5—Creditors, the debtor, and the estate, which deals with the status of creditors and the nature and documentation of their claims; the rights and obligations of the debtor; and

the handling of the estate, the body of assets and rights the
debtor brings into the proceedings.

- Chapter 7—Liquidation, which is divided into subchapters
  governing the appointment and role of the trustee, the process
  of liquidation, and special provisions for the liquidation of
  stockbrokers, commodity brokers, and clearing banks.
- Chapter 9—Municipal bankruptcy.
- Chapter 11—Corporate reorganization, including a separate
  subchapter on railroad reorganization.
- Chapter 12—Bankruptcy of family farms or fishermen.
- Chapter 13—Individual reorganization.
- Chapter 15—Ancillary and other cross-border cases, dealing
  with international bankruptcy issues such as the rights of foreign representatives and creditors in U.S. courts, recognition
  of foreign proceedings, cooperation with foreign courts, and
  joint U.S.-foreign cases.

In the rest of this book, we will consider all of the above but Chapters 9,
12, 13, and 15. Chapters 1, 3, and 5 are of general applicability or otherwise touch upon threshold issues of a bankruptcy case. Therefore, these
sections will be the focus of the following two chapters, after which liquidation and reorganization will be considered in Chapter 4.

1.3.3 Terminology

There are several phrases and terms used frequently in the discussion to
follow of which the reader, especially anyone with a non-business back-
ground, should be aware:

- "Claimant" is a generic term for any party with a claim or
  interest in the bankruptcy case. This includes the traditional
  creditor, but also may include parties such as judgment
  holders and lessors or other contractual counterparties. This
  term will be used throughout in a generally interchangeable
  manner with the usual reference to the "creditor" in order to
  denote this broader definition. "Creditor" will be used where

the specific context normally arises only in a direct, consensual arrangement between a borrower and a lender.

- "Collateral" is property of the debtor that is pledged to a creditor as security for the obligation. This establishes what is known as a "security interest" in the collateral in favor of the creditor to whom it is granted (and who becomes a "secured creditor"; see below).
- "Estate" refers to the body of property belonging to the debtor, all of which is subject to court oversight and administration.
- "Perfection" refers to the acts required of a creditor to provide notice and documentation of its security interest in specific collateral. The specific requirements depend upon the nature of the collateral in question and the laws of the state where the transaction originated or where the collateral is located. Frequently, this entails filing a "financing statement" or other appropriate documentation detailing the collateral subject to the security interest with the appropriate state body or official, who records or indexes the document for public notice. *Perfecting the security interest is necessary in order to be considered a secured creditor in the bankruptcy proceeding.*
- "Petition" is the physical bankruptcy filing. The Bankruptcy Code distinguishes in certain circumstances between claims and actions occurring prior to the bankruptcy, which are referred to as "pre-petition," and those occurring after the bankruptcy begins, and which are therefore referred to as "post-petition."
- "Priority" refers to the position in the bankruptcy hierarchy occupied by a given kind of claim. Some claims are entitled to higher priority than others, and as we will see later some arise during the bankruptcy proceedings and are given "superpriority" status.
- "Secured creditor" means a creditor who has perfected a security interest, almost always in accordance with a signed security agreement between the creditor and the debtor, in specific collateral of the debtor.

- "Trustee" refers to the situation in which, upon court order, a trustee is appointed to operate the debtor company during the bankruptcy proceeding. In most cases, this step is not taken and the debtor retains its management team (or a new team is appointed); this represents the "debtor-in-possession" norm of bankruptcy. The term "trustee" also should be distinguished from "U.S. trustee," a permanent feature of bankruptcy administration intended to provide oversight of the case, but not to run or direct the affairs of the company as a "trustee" would. The role of the U.S. trustee is discussed in the text below.
- "Unsecured creditor" refers to a creditor who either did not perfect a security interest in specific collateral or who does not have an interest in collateral to begin with. Trade creditors would be a common example of the latter.
- From time to time a party's identity as a participant in a specific kind of transaction results in the use of phrases ending in "-ee" or "-or," for example a lessee or lessor. The general rule to keep in mind is that the party granting the interest or taking the action in question is the "-or" party, while the party receiving the benefit is the "-ee" party (e.g., a lessor gives a leasehold interest to a lessee, or a transferor transfers property to a transferee).

With these basic concepts in mind, we turn now to the beginning of a bankruptcy case and the various procedural issues and initial decisions surrounding the filing of a petition.

CHAPTER 2

Getting Started

Filing Decisions and Effects

This chapter considers generally applicable issues of bankruptcy administration and several threshold issues of a bankruptcy case, including issues of eligibility and where and when to file. We will also briefly touch upon the matter of involuntary bankruptcies, a relative rarity in today's practice but nevertheless a legitimate alternative under the circumstances delineated in the statute. Also, once a case is filed, certain judicial procedures are immediately implemented, notably the automatic stay. Familiarity with these basics is a must for anyone seeking insight into the operation of bankruptcy law and practice.

2.1 Commencement of the Case

2.1.1 Filing Mechanics and Eligibility Issues

We will begin our discussion with the more prevalent situation of the voluntary petition in bankruptcy. The Code states simply, "A voluntary case under a chapter of this title is commenced by the filing with the bankruptcy court of a petition under such chapter by an entity that may be a debtor under such chapter."[1] The operative phrases "entity" and "debtor" both are keyed to the definition of "person," which includes an "individual, partnership, and corporation."[2] The specific debtors eligible to file under each of the Code's chapters, which for our purposes will be limited to Chapters 7 and 11, are identified separately.[3] Under that provision, with three exceptions for railroads, enumerated financial institutions, and foreign insurance companies, any person may file a Chapter 7 petition. In turn, any person eligible to file under Chapter 7, other than stock or commodity brokers, uninsured state banks, and "multilateral clearing organizations," may file under Chapter 11.[4] It is important to note that the Code now imposes new procedural requirements in small business bankruptcies, a topic considered in more depth later in this text's Chapter 5.

Battlegrounds

1. Case conversion: Either debtor or claimants may seek conversion of the case from Chapter 7 to Chapter 11, or vice versa. May be useful as leverage. See 2.1.2.

2. Venue: Relative elasticity of filing requirements may facilitate forum shopping. See 2.1.3.

3. Timing: No absolute insolvency condition is stated in the Code. Thus, there is wide discretion as to the precise point at which a distressed debtor may file, but significant implications for recovery may be associated with the debtor's financial condition at the date of filing. See 2.1.4.

4. The automatic stay: Protects debtors from any and all collection efforts; creditors may seek relief. See 2.1.5.1 and following.

5. Entities included or excluded in case: Recall that an organization need not include all parts of its "family." Because it is not a separate and explicit part of the process, and is not a common feature, the issue is treated in Chapter 5 of this text. But the timing of any such considerations would occur close to the time of the bankruptcy filing. Likewise, small business bankruptcy considerations, where applicable, are discussed in Chapter 5.

2.1.2 The Choice of Chapter 7 or Chapter 11

One question to be addressed by the debtor at this point is whether to choose liquidation under Chapter 7 or reorganization under Chapter 11, assuming that the basic eligibility tests are met for both. There is no general rule that applies to this decision, although certainly a clear-eyed estimation of the value of the business as a going concern, indeed whether it is a going concern at all under any objective measure, would be a starting point. But assuming that there is no question regarding the business' fundamental viability and going concern value, Chapter 11 is almost always preferable and usually more beneficial to virtually all parties involved, given the opportunity it provides to realign the financial structure of the debtor company and possibly still permit at least some long-term recovery on pre-petition obligations.

Moreover, the decision to choose either a liquidation or reorganization is not in itself conclusively determinative or permanent. All parties, debtors and creditors alike, should be aware that the Code permits conversion from one type of proceeding to the other.[5] As a preliminary matter, it is important to understand that conversion does not "restart" the bankruptcy. In other words, the date the original petition was filed remains the effective date for the case for purposes of the automatic stay and pre- and post-petition actions and operations of the debtor, topics discussed later in this text. Converting from Chapter 7 to Chapter 11 requires merely that the case was not previously converted from a Chapter 11 proceeding, while converting from a Chapter 11 case is permitted unless a trustee has been appointed (in other words, the debtor must be the debtor-in-possession), the case was involuntary, or the case already was converted to Chapter 11 on motion by someone other than the debtor.

The latter provision also confirms that it is not only the debtor who may seek conversion; claimants may do so as well, but there is a critical distinction that operates as something of a strategic gateway: Assuming the threshold requirements for conversion are met, the debtor has the absolute right to convert, while other parties must seek court approval. Thus, while conversion is available to either side, the necessity of court intervention on behalf of creditors and other claimants in effect means that conversion is relatively more of a weapon in the hands of the debtor. Depending on the circumstances of the particular case, the debtor might seek to use its conversion rights as leverage under either type of proceeding (though usually one would expect this approach to be of more value in reorganization, with the implicit or explicit threat of conversion to a Chapter 7 liquidation).

Careful reading of the conditions for conversion, though, will satisfy the reader that this is a weapon with limited ammunition. Once converted from Chapter 11, a Chapter 7 case cannot be converted back to Chapter 11 voluntarily by the debtor. Cases arising under Chapter 7, however, may be converted from Chapter 11 to Chapter 7 if the *debtor* initiated the original conversion, but no additional conversions would be permitted thereafter. Note that this also means that a claimant who succeeded in forcing a conversion from Chapter 7 to Chapter 11 (itself a relatively unlikely scenario) cannot thereby defeat the debtor's right to reconvert to Chapter 7. The net result of these provisions means that the debtor cannot avail itself of conversion an unlimited number of times. But the use or, more likely, the threat of conversion may still be a potent tool for both debtors and creditors.

2.1.3 Where to File

The fact that this topic is titled as it is, and even considered at all, might seem strange at first glance. After all, one would expect to file any legal action in one's home region. Moreover, the Judicial Code provides that a bankruptcy petition may be filed in the district court where the "domicile, residence, principal place of business in the United States, or principal assets" of the debtor were located "for the one hundred eighty days immediately preceding" the filing, or where there is a pending case involving an affiliate, general partner, or partnership in which the debtor has an interest.[6] Even granting that businesses commonly have far-flung operations, assets, and places of business, the import of this statute seems to be clear enough and consistent with a common sense notion of where cases are, or should be, commenced.

But this is the law with which we are concerned, and we must remember what Dickens said about the law. In fact, there are a number of gray areas lurking in this formulation that permit or even facilitate the practice of forum shopping. In a non-judgmental sense, the term means only that a petitioner chooses the most appropriate forum for the case. But experience has shown that forum shopping often results in abuse of the system, as petitioners can seek not just a convenient location, but rather attempt to find one whose judicial reputation leans in the petitioner's favor. The choice of a bankruptcy forum is not exempt from this reality.

Let us consider the relevant issues. We will begin with the phrase "principal place of business," which, of course, is the only term in the opening clause applicable to a business debtor. Note that either the company's headquarters or the location of the company's largest office or plant could be considered the "principal place of business" on a given set of facts, but in most cases the location of the company's CEO is taken to be its place of business for purposes such as this.[7] Now consider: A company's new CEO is from Florida, while the business is headquartered in a cold weather location. The new CEO does not wish to relocate. Therefore, the company sets up an office near the CEO's home in Florida, and that office becomes the "principal place of business," even though the rest of the company's operations take place at its original site.

Many businesses, especially ones of any size, make similar decisions or simply maintain a number of different operations centers. Or the issue might arise in conjunction with a merger, in which both parties have multiple business locations and different "headquarters" locations at which their pre-merger CEOs were located. Any such site could be chosen as the place of business. Now consider the possibility of a strategic relocation: We know the company isn't doing well, but we also know the judges in our district are notoriously creditor-friendly. Therefore, we move our CEO/executive team to a different location, wait the requisite period of time to establish "domicile," and then file the bankruptcy petition in that location.

Likewise, the "principal assets" test can be manipulated by an unscrupulous or merely opportunistic debtor. It is certainly true that a business cannot always rearrange its asset base for this purpose, but it is possible and may require only minute shifts in investment here and there to accomplish. For example, suppose the Rotten Seafood Company operates a fleet of fishing vessels at various locations up and down the Eastern seaboard. No given location represents a majority of the company's assets, but one does at least have a plurality of 30%. Unfortunately, this jurisdiction is not debtor-friendly, and Rotten wants to be sure to be able to file in a different district in which roughly 25% of its assets reside. A few boat sales in one and purchases in another, or perhaps the simple movement of the boats from one to the other and their re-registration in the new location, and we have accomplished our purpose.

The "affiliate" test arguably is even more permissive. As a rule, when companies increase in size, the number of their subsidiaries increases in tandem. In many instances, each of these subsidiaries is separately incorporated, even though commonly owned by the corporate parent. For purposes of bankruptcy venue, each of the subsidiaries is an affiliate, so that the corporate parent could choose which one would file first, and then use that filing as the platform on which the rest of the subsidiaries and the parent would file later. And, of course, it is possible that the parent might exclude some of the subsidiaries from the filing, though any attempt to "hide" assets from the bankruptcy by shifting title or the physical location of property might be subject to challenge as an avoidable transfer (see the text in Chapter 3). But if just one other subsidiary exists, the corporate parent can claim affiliate status and use that subsidiary's location to initiate its own petition. This was the mechanism by which both Enron (headquartered in Houston) and GM (headquarters and presence in Michigan) filed in New York; in the former case, a subsidiary was used, while in the latter the bankruptcy of a company-owned dealer was the mode of entry.

Why was New York a magnet for these companies? Professor Lynn LoPucki, in multiyear investigations of bankruptcy cases, concludes that judicial approaches and proclivities and other jurisdiction-specific practices influence case proceedings and their ultimate resolution.[8] In separate work, he asserts that New York's legal infrastructure, and in particular its bankruptcy bar, requires a heavy caseload to sustain, leading to an assertive and competitive stance in acquiring cases.[9] And in his analysis, New York tends to be debtor-friendly, permitting extensions of the exclusivity period applicable to the development of the plan of reorganization (see Chapter 4) that allow the debtor to remain in control of the proceedings (and avoid paying its outstanding obligations, by the way). But even worse, in what some might term irony or poetic justice, New York cases often result in lost economic value to both claimants and debtors alike, in the latter case leaving the debtor companies too weak to compete effectively following their reorganization.

The point of this discussion is not necessarily to condemn legitimate choice of forum decisions in general, but to highlight the issues involved so that both sides of a bankruptcy case can understand their implications. Clearly, abusive or opportunistic filings are problematic if one is concerned with an orderly and economically just distribution to the debtor's claimants, and reform efforts may reasonably focus on such behavior. There are, however, legitimate uses to which the vague statutory language reasonably can be put, and debtors should not be wary of legitimate resort to their use. On the other hand, claimants monitoring a debtor's activities and observing patterns of this kind can anticipate where they will lead and act accordingly. Even if a debtor establishes a presence in a jurisdiction using one of the methods described here, claimants may be able to challenge that court's assertion of jurisdiction on grounds of abuse or convenience.[10] Ultimately, the message of this section is that venue is a flexible construct that both debtors and creditors need to understand in order to seek the best possible outcome and protect their interests.

2.1.4 When to File

The question of when to file is one of the most significant decisions a business can make. There can be legitimate concerns for the reputation of the business and the maintenance of relationships, but a good public relations strategy can overcome many of these obstacles.[11] Another issue that cannot be overlooked is the significant cost associated with the bankruptcy process.[12]

There is also general awareness, and perhaps some corresponding trepidation, in the business community about the relatively low rate of successful reorganization cases. Historically, commentators have put the number somewhere around 15–20%, although a report issued by the Executive Office for United States Trustees during the 1990s raised that number to about 25%, with approximately 35% of the cases dismissed and an additional 35% converted.[13] More recent work by Professors Elizabeth Warren and Jay Westbrook suggests that the earlier estimates included many cases in which the debtor was too weak to save, thus distorting the results. In other words, the starting point of the comparisons, total filings, includes any case ever filed regardless of the actual status of the debtor organization, including those that might charitably be called dead on arrival. If these cases were excluded, Warren and Westbrook estimate that as many as 65–70% of reorganization cases in which a plan actually is promulgated eventually succeed in achieving confirmation, the putative hallmark of a successful reorganization.[14] Thus, while not a perfect score, companies that actually are viable and able to initiate a plan of reorganization probably have a reasonably good chance of succeeding. And we must not lose sight of the alternatives, liquidation or continuing deterioration of the business, in deciding whether to attempt reorganization.

Unfortunately, there is a body of empirical research suggesting that many businesses in fact wait too long to file. Pioneering work by Professors Donald Hambrick and Richard D'Aveni documented what is known as the "downward spiral" phenomenon, in which the business becomes progressively weaker and continues to see its asset base diminish, only to file when little is left to save.[15] There can be many reasons for the decision to avoid filing for as long as possible, including personal concern for one's reputation or the prospect of eventual displacement in a bankruptcy proceeding.[16] There is also some debate in academia whether the bankruptcy system itself fosters outcomes of this sort by providing incentives to delay filing and, in the meantime, undertake riskier strategies in an effort to turn the business around.[17] If we view bankruptcy as providing an option on the firm's asset value, then any failing business with an asset value less than total indebtedness could simply be turned over to the creditors in bankruptcy with no more than the loss of already depleted equity value. If, on the other hand, the asset value can be increased to a level in excess of total indebtedness, the surplus belongs to the equity owners. On this view, if there is a chance to drive the value of the firm's assets above that of its indebtedness, the prospect of imminent bankruptcy may lead to the adoption of high-risk, high-reward strategies that either return the business to solvency, redounding to the benefit of the equity owners, or fail and further deplete the firm's resource base, harming only the creditors at the margin.

The latter scenario broadly depicts the premise of what is known as prospect theory, in which the context, or framing, of the problem we face affects our posture toward risk and thus our decisions.[18] If we are losing, we tend to be more willing to accept risk than when we are winning and wish simply to conserve our capital. For example, suppose I offer you a choice between accepting a guaranteed payout of $200 or a lottery ticket with a 25% chance of winning $1000 and a 75% chance of winning nothing. Alternatively, suppose instead that I offer you a choice between a guaranteed loss of $200 or a gamble that offers a 25% chance of losing $1000 but a 75% chance of losing nothing. When I conduct this thought experiment in my MBA classes, probably 90% or more of the responses consistently favor the guaranteed payout in the first scenario and the gamble in the second. But notice that on an expected value basis, we should prefer exactly the opposite in each case: The lottery in the first scenario is worth $250, while in the second the gamble can be expected to cost us $250. We become risk averse when we should be willing to take chances, and we become risk seeking when we should avoid it. Studies also have extended similar reasoning to business investment decisions outside the bankruptcy context, in which incentives provided by options-based compensation seem to result in the adoption of high-risk projects.[19]

If we translate these insights back into a bankruptcy setting, considering the effects of commonly adopted options contracts as well, we can begin to understand the dynamics involved in the downward spiral phenomenon. We are in a loss-framed scenario, and the best course of action seems to be to take the big gamble to pull the company out of its tailspin. But if these sorts of risky bets fail, as is common, and the business ends up in a protracted stage of decline, equity is likely to be completely wiped out even in an eventual reorganization, much less a liquidation. It would seem to make more sense, then, to attempt to preserve as much residual equity value as possible. All the more so, in fact, if management itself is armed with an equity position in the firm, for then the rewards and incentives of equity recovery become personal gain, not just a matter of fiduciary duty to shareholders at large.

Given this reasoning, I conducted a study investigating whether the extent of managerial stock ownership increased the solvency levels of firms filing for reorganization. This turned out not to be the case, and in fact the companies filing before the onset of significant insolvency tended to be those whose managers had only limited equity positions.[20] The evidence suggested that filing often is delayed when substantial equity stakes are held by incumbent management, potentially resulting in harm to the long-run prospects, or even the existence, of the distressed business. As we have just seen, there can be psychological reasons for this, or the decision can be a result of the common perception of the fate of equity in bankruptcy and the desire to spare shareholders (and share-owning management itself) that experience. But given the findings for low equity holdings, the effect of stock ownership seems to be to induce hesitation to file, whatever the underlying rationale may be. Bankruptcy apparently is perceived as a risk to accumulated wealth that should be avoided at all costs.

Although every case is different, officers and directors instead should consider the question of when to file in light of both corporate law and the dynamics of the reorganization process. From a legal standpoint, the availability of the reorganization process to corporate debtors arguably creates an enforceable fiduciary duty to file *before* a downward spiral is underway or irreversible. As mentioned in Chapter 1 above, existing case law in fact suggests that "in the zone of insolvency" the focal point of fiduciary duty shifts in favor of the firm's creditors.[21] Given that creditors do not normally participate in gains from successful risky strategies, filing delays arising from the pursuit of such strategies, in the hope that a "home run" will be hit so that bankruptcy can be avoided, arguably constitutes a breach of this duty. This conclusion becomes even clearer if we consider that the failure of turnaround strategies in a distressed firm is likely to imperil shareholder interests as well.

The dynamics of the bankruptcy process also tend to support early filing. Research evidence suggests that when filing occurs at early stages of decline, equity tends to participate in bankruptcy distributions to a greater extent than would hold under normal distribution scenarios (i.e., where the rule of "absolute priority" is followed, paying the first priority claimants in full before making any distribution to the next lower priority claimants, and so on down the line).[22] To some extent, outcomes such as these reflect the mechanical realities of securing plan confirmation, a topic to be considered later, and it is also true that the studies showing equity participation also indicate that the difference between an "absolute priority" distribution and the observed distributions of the studies tends to be fairly small. But once again, the message of the available evidence seems to be that everyone is better off if distress is resolved early in the process of decline: Creditors can be offered more and shareholders may be able to participate in the reorganization to a greater extent than is likely in late-stage decline bankruptcies. At the very least, filing sooner rather than later in the face of decline increases the likelihood of successful reorganization, as Warren and Westbrook's evidence suggests.[23] And if the concern is displacement, I would argue that a management team perceived as taking proactive steps to resolve financial distress is more likely to be retained than one that allows the company to undergo a downward spiral.

Strange as it may seem, the Code actually does not require insolvency as a prerequisite to filing. While the Code defines the term for specific purposes we will delineate later in this book, recourse to the various bankruptcy procedures of the Code is conditioned only on the basis of the debtor's *identity*, not on the debtor's financial condition.[24] Thus, at least in theory, a perfectly solvent company such as Microsoft, with its eleven-figure cash balance, could walk into bankruptcy court and file a petition. However, there is some existing legal precedent for the notion that a solvent company filing a petition in bankruptcy is not filing in good faith and thus is subject to dismissal.[25] But this holding emerged in the context of a company facing significant antitrust liability and proposing a plan that called only for the antitrust claimants to accept less than the full value of their claims. The court's decision relied substantially on an equity basis in imposing a "good faith filing" requirement, and explicitly stated that it was not holding that a company must await the rendering of a massive judgment against it before entering Chapter 11. The example of Johns-Manville, the company that filed a Chapter 11 petition in order to rationalize its outstanding asbestos claims, was distinguished on the basis that it represented a case in which the debtor was found to have a compelling need to seek reorganization. What the decision seems to mean, then, is that a solvent company cannot opportunistically avail itself of bankruptcy protection for the obvious and sole purpose of eliminating an adverse judgment or the valid claim of a specific creditor. A still-solvent company, though, may have a good faith basis for filing if it can establish that circumstances exist that, if not dealt with in reorganization, would substantially impair its business prospects and operations and/or lead to liquidation.

In sum, as we have just seen, it is often advisable for a debtor to file before insolvency reaches irreversible levels, and perhaps even while solvent if specific facts support the filing. Remember that the Code itself, if limited to its express language, does not forbid this from happening, and indeed no showing of minor, moderate, or significant insolvency is necessary to file a legitimate petition. The decision to file, then, represents a business decision, but one that should be taken with the interests of all stakeholders in mind. As we have discussed, fiduciary standards would seem to impose a duty to consider the implications of extended decline, and legal authority supports consideration of creditor interests in evaluation of the prospects of the business. Generally, it is better to file before the company has substantially depleted its resource base and cannot be successfully reorganized or provide adequate recovery to stakeholders as a group.

2.1.5 Effect of Filing

The date of the filing is important for both administrative and procedural reasons. Administratively, within 14 days after the filing the debtor must furnish a variety of disclosures and materials with the court. These include, of course, financial statements, but also lists of contracts, equity ownership, and in Chapter 11 cases, a schedule of the 20 largest unsecured creditors and their contact information. Names and addresses of all creditors also are required for notice purposes.[26] Finally, evidence of authority to act is necessary; for corporations, this will entail documentation of board action authorizing the corporation to file the petition.

Upon filing, the bankruptcy case, regardless of the specific chapter election, is subject to the administrative oversight of the U.S. Trustee, a separate division of the Department of Justice. The duties of the U.S. Trustee are enumerated by statute,[27] and from time to time are referred to herein when a particular action is reserved to or required of the U.S. Trustee. The essential purpose of the U.S. Trustee is to ensure that fraud and abuse are avoided and that the case proceeds as expeditiously as possible. One of the first acts of the trustee is to organize the meeting of creditors, and perhaps a meeting of equity holders,[28] at which the U.S. Trustee presides. The debtor is examined under oath with respect to the nature and extent of its obligations, together with any other matters pertinent to the case.

Procedurally, the date of filing is important because it establishes a "red line" against which all past and future interactions are judged. First and foremost is the initiation of the automatic stay as of the filing date, which is the weapon debtors are provided to shield themselves from postpetition collection activities. It is this provision that underlies the popular terminology of "relief" or "protection" from creditors, for any and all such activities are prohibited and subject to substantial sanctions if the court finds a violation.

2.1.5.1 The Automatic Stay

Let us examine the stay more closely. Table 2.1 presents the pertinent language of the Code, which establishes the specific contours of the stay.[29] Notice the breadth of this provision, covering a variety of different actions, some of which may seem to be a natural extension of the legal arrangement between the parties. After all, if you and I undertake a contractual agreement obligating you to pay me a certain amount at certain

Table 2.1. Section 362: Automatic Stay

(a) Except as provided in subsection (b)...a petition filed under Section 301...operates as a stay, applicable to all entities, of—

1) the commencement or continuation, including the issuance or employment of process, of a judicial, administrative, or other action or proceeding against the debtor that was or could have been commenced before the commencement of the case under this title, or to recover a claim against the debtor that arose before the commencement of the case...;

2) the enforcement, against the debtor or against property of the estate, of a judgment obtained before the commencement of the case...;

3) any act to obtain possession of property of the estate or of property from the estate or to exercise control over property of the estate;

4) any act to create, perfect, or enforce any lien against property of the estate;

5) any act to create, perfect, or enforce against property of the debtor any lien to the extent that such lien secures a claim that arose before the commencement of the case...;

6) any act to collect, assess, or recover a claim against the debtor that arose before the commencement of the case...;

7) the setoff of any debt owing to the debtor that arose before the commencement of the case...;

8) the commencement of continuation of a proceeding before the United States Tax Court...;

(b) The filing of a petition...does not operate as a stay—

1) ...of the commencement or continuation of a criminal action or proceeding against the debtor;

2) [of certain domestic actions];...

7) ...of the exercise by a repo participant or financial participant of any contractual right...under any security agreement...forming a part of or related to any repurchase agreement, or of any contractual right...to offset or net out any termination value, payment amount, or other transfer obligation...;...

10) ...of any act by a lessor to the debtor under a lease of non-residential real property that has terminated by the expiration of the stated terms of the lease before the commencement of or during a case under this title to obtain possession of such property;

11) ...of the presentment of a negotiable instrument and the giving of notice of and protesting dishonor of such an instrument;...

17) ...of the exercise by a swap participant or financial participant of any contractual right... under any security agreement or arrangement...or of any contractual right...to offset or net out any termination value, payment amount, or other transfer obligation...;

times, the obligation exists as a matter of law and it would seem to be part and parcel of that arrangement for me to do whatever is necessary to tie up loose ends or otherwise formalize the contract. In fact, doing so is necessary as a matter of law for me to *protect* my interest in your performance (a process known as "perfection," which will be discussed later). But the Code does not view our contract in this light. Instead, it views the world and the affairs of the debtor through the prism of the filing, and distinguishes those acts occurring prior to the petition from those occurring afterwards. As far as the Code is concerned, my rights are frozen as of the date of the petition, since the filing of the petition establishes a technically new creature I did not contract with. Thus, if I have not "dotted i's and crossed t's," it's my problem; I still have a contract with you and you still owe me the stipulated sum, but my right to collect that from you in bankruptcy is dependent upon not only the arrangement between us but also my completion of whatever steps were necessary to protect my interests *prior* to your filing the petition, up to and including perfection of any security interest.

Turning to the statute itself, notice first that the stay applies to "all entities." This means not only private creditors, but also courts, collection agencies, judgment holders, lessors, and indeed anyone with any kind of claim pending against the debtor. Clearly, the firm's private creditors will be aware of the petition, certainly if they are scheduled on the initial filing. But let us suppose I supply your company's letterhead and bill you monthly. The amount owed in any given month is relatively small, particularly in light of your company's other obligations, and I am not scheduled among the largest 20 creditors. Perhaps you even legitimately forgot about my bill. During the month you file your bankruptcy petition. When the payment is not received I contact you to ask when I might expect it. Have I violated the stay, given that I did not know of the petition? The answer is yes; Section 362(a)(6) usually is interpreted as barring direct communication with the debtor, particularly collection calls. And for purposes of this analysis, knowledge of the filing is not the issue under the stay. All actions to collect are barred, and those attempting to collect violate the stay. Violations are subject to various penalties, and here my lack of knowledge of your bankruptcy petition would bear upon the question of my penalty, given that my violation was not intentional. But the protection of the stay itself is absolute.

Before we consider other hypothetical examples, note also that the stay is subject to certain exceptions. Those relevant to a corporate bankruptcy, and which are more likely to arise, also are reproduced in Table 2.1. First and foremost, criminal actions are not stayed. Thus, if Endrun, Inc., engages in systemic deception, can it seek bankruptcy protection in order to defeat those it defrauded? Not if criminal charges are brought; such proceedings may continue notwithstanding the stay. Civil fraud claims, unfortunately, will still be subject to the stay. Notice that like this situation, the other exceptions are very specific, and while they may indeed arise, they are not subject to much interpretation or generalization. Only subparagraph (b)(11), dealing with the presentation of negotiable instruments such as checks, might be relatively more routine, but note that the action permitted goes only to presentment and the protest of dishonor. It does not authorize the claimant to collect the amount owed.

To better understand the breadth of the stay and some of the common actions that are permissible or impermissible, we will examine a few hypothetical circumstances involving a claimant's actions vis-à-vis a debtor. We have already seen that calling the debtor to seek payment is a violation of the stay. Consider the following:

- ABC, Inc., owes Big Bank $2 million, and signs a security agreement giving the bank an interest in its accounts receivable. With the agreement in hand, Big Bank puts the paperwork in its files and takes no further action until notified of ABC's bankruptcy. Big Bank then perfects its security interest by sending notice of the agreement to the appropriate state office. Notice that Big Bank has not attempted to collect on the debt, and thus has not violated the stay to that extent. But its action in attempting to perfect its interest does violate Sections 362(a)(4) and (5).

- Let us suppose that Big Bank realizes its error with the security interest and does not attempt perfection. Instead, the bank turns to the compensating balances of ABC held at the bank as part of the financing agreement, deducting the $2 million owed from ABC accounts. This is a clear violation of Section 362(a)(7), which forbids such setoffs.

- Now suppose that Risky Business was party to an interest rate swap with Paws, Inc., in which Paws held cash collateral provided by Risky Business. The agreement between the parties authorizes Paws to exercise a right of setoff in the event of default by Risky Business. Risky Business defaults and files bankruptcy. Paws executes on the agreement by exercising its right of setoff against Risky Business. This action would be permissible under Section 362(b)(17).

- I lease an office building to your company. The lease expires on August 15. You do not make your final half-month's payment on August 1, and file bankruptcy on August 5. Not receiving payment, upon expiration of the lease I initiate action to regain possession of the premises. This violates Section 362(a)(6), and possibly (a)(3) if my action is intended to assume control of any of your property left in the building in order to satisfy the unpaid lease obligation. If, on the other hand, you file on August 20, my actions, at least to the extent limited to regaining possession of the premises, are permitted by 362(a)(6). Note that I still cannot seize any property you leave behind in satisfaction of any unpaid lease obligations.

As this selection of hypotheticals suggests, there are a number of ways in which a creditor or other claimant can run afoul of the automatic stay, and relatively few in which the actions in question will be permissible. As indicated above, the stay is intended to give relief to the debtor, but operationally it is designed to ensure that any enforcement actions are undertaken subject to court supervision and with the consent, where necessary, of other claimants. To that extent, the stay represents an integral part of the system by which bankruptcy law facilitates an orderly disposition of the debtor's obligations, without favor to a particular creditor who might be able to grab the debtor's property faster than others. It is imperative, then, that any claimant tread carefully with respect to enforcement actions; if you believe a party with which your organization has dealings is at risk of bankruptcy, carefully monitor its status to ensure that your actions are not undertaken after a petition is filed. And most importantly in such situations, act quickly (and almost always it is better to perfect simultaneously with the close of the transaction giving rise to the interest; post-transaction perfection is risky, even if undertaken pre-petition, for reasons we will investigate later) if you believe bankruptcy risk is increasing, especially where documenting or perfecting your claim is concerned. Remember that once the petition is filed, your rights are fixed even if you haven't completed these steps.

2.1.5.2 Relief from the Stay; Adequate Protection

Suppose now that you have complied with the terms of the stay, and have no intention of doing anything that would constitute a violation. Suppose also that you are a secured creditor, but you are afraid that the value of the property securing your claim will deteriorate, leaving you with less than that to which you are entitled. Other than letting the bankruptcy case play out, and thereby risking the value of your collateral, the Code permits you as a secured creditor (note that unsecured creditors do not have the right to seek relief under this provision) to petition the bankruptcy court for relief from the stay, and specifies four different remedies the court may order:[30]

- *Termination*, which ends the stay with respect to the specific collateral at issue, but only from the date of the order. Prior violations of the stay remain subject to sanction.
- *Annulment*, representing a retroactive lifting of the stay, in effect treating the stay as if it had never taken effect. Prior violations therefore are excused. This remedy typically arises only in extreme circumstances, often involving some form of procedural or systemic abuse by the debtor.
- *Modification*, which limits the claimant's rights to the collateral but permits specified actions otherwise barred by the stay. This will, of course, be case-specific, but might entail perfection actions otherwise barred or perhaps the retention of the collateral (but not its sale).
- *Conditioning*, in which the stay remains in effect subject only to the debtor's compliance with specific requirements.

What must the claimant establish in order to seek relief from the stay? In most cases, one of two grounds will be asserted: either that just cause exists, which as suggested in our introductory hypothetical might be that the creditor lacks "adequate protection,"[31] or that the debtor has no equity in the property in question and that the property as a result is not necessary for an effective reorganization under Chapter 11.[32]

Turning first to relief for cause, it is important to understand that the Code does not specify or define circumstances that constitute "cause," and thus a variety of facts could give rise to a valid argument. Only prior case law in the jurisdiction governing the case might serve as guidance or limit the claimant's options. The one clear specification of the Code, though, applies to cases in which a secured creditor lacks adequate protection in the collateral subject to the stay. The debtor bears the burden of proof in establishing the existence of adequate protection, thus simplifying the creditor's assertion.[33] Assuming that the debtor cannot prove that adequate protection exists, the court may respond by requiring periodic cash payments by the debtor, a substitute or additional lien in other property of the debtor, or "such other relief...as will result in the realization...of the indubitable equivalent of [the creditor's] interest in such property."[34] Needless to say, there is always controversy concerning the precise meaning of "indubitable equivalent," but the purpose of the provision is more to provide a general standard than to define or condition the remedy in question. In raising the question or defending against a motion in which the matter is raised, the parties involved must be prepared to address what the value of the creditor's interest is and how that interest is or is not being protected. If the court finds that adequate protection does not exist, and does not believe that cash or liens will suffice, the stay will be lifted and the creditor may proceed against the collateral, subject to any terms imposed by the court in a modification remedy as discussed above.

In the alternative, the creditor may seek relief from the stay by arguing that the debtor lacks equity in the property and that the property is not necessary to an effective reorganization.[35] Unlike motions for relief on grounds of adequate protection, the creditor bears the burden of proof on the question of the debtor's equity in the collateral, which makes this assertion somewhat more difficult to carry. And as will be discussed below, questions of valuation necessarily are contentious and subject to varying interpretations or opinions.

But as this suggests, the creditor also must establish that the property is not necessary to an effective reorganization. This marks a distinction between liquidation and reorganization cases, for in the former only a finding of no equity is sufficient; reorganization is not the point of the proceeding. In reorganization, though, even if the debtor has no equity in the property, that property may still form the basis of the debtor's operations and therefore be necessary to a successful reorganization. Only if both conditions are satisfied will relief from the stay be granted in a Chapter 11 case.

By now, it should be apparent that lifting the stay is a matter of some complexity and uncertainty. It is certainly possible to gain relief and proceed against the collateral, and in most cases adequate protection will serve as the preferred route to this outcome. But the foregoing discussion should indicate that relief from the stay is not ordered of right, and that there are many points of conflict where the motion for relief might fail. Thus, in most instances, claimants should be prepared to abide by the terms of the stay. Note again that we are dealing with an issue applicable to the status of a *secured* creditor; unsecured creditors do not have this remedy available to them.

2.2 Involuntary Petitions

Most of the time, bankruptcy is a voluntary act of a debtor. However, the Code does provide for involuntary bankruptcy, that is, bankruptcy that is declared at the behest of claimants. The plural is used here because Section 303 requires that the involuntary petition be initiated by at least three claimants holding, in the aggregate, at least $13,475 (as of August 1, 2007 and subject to periodic revision) in unsecured claims that are not contingent or subject to legitimate dispute as to amount or nature. The language of statute implies that these claimants may include undersecured creditors (see below, in "Priorities") as well as general unsecured claimants ("$13,475 more than the value of any lien on property of the debtor securing such claims"). If there are fewer than 12 such claimants, only one is necessary to initiate the involuntary petition. The three-claimant requirement is intended to protect larger debtors from a disgruntled claimant who would otherwise be unable to convince others to support the involuntary petition.

The involuntary petition can be filed only under Chapter 7 or Chapter 11. If Chapter 7 is elected, the Code gives the court authority to order the appointment of an interim trustee for the debtor pending the court's acceptance of the petition.[36] Otherwise, until such time the debtor is entitled to continue its operations, and has full use of its assets, including the right to sell or lease all or any portion of its property.[37] The debtor is deemed to have accepted the involuntary petition if the debtor does not dispute its contents.[38] If the debtor does so, however, perhaps by raising non-bankruptcy defenses or disputing the claims in question, the court is to accept the involuntary petition only if the debtor is not paying its undisputed debts as they come due. The purpose of these provisions is clear: Debtors are afforded an opportunity to defend themselves against unjust or spurious claims that would drive them into bankruptcy unwillingly.

Given the nature of and requirements for involuntary petitions, it should come as no surprise that the number of involuntary bankruptcies is almost always negligible. Suppose, though, that a claimant has a legitimate concern about the debtor's performance (perhaps generally paying debts as they come due, but not completely regularly, for example), financial condition, or collateral value, especially if the debtor does not file bankruptcy of its own volition and indeed might be expected to delay any such decision. If recourse to the involuntary bankruptcy process seems impractical or is unavailable, then other than some kind of negotiation with the debtor to iron out differences a claimant can only resort to non-bankruptcy legal remedies, such as declaring default at the earliest possible moment under any existing agreement, seizing collateral where permitted, etc. Note that this should not be construed as a suggestion to harass the debtor unjustifiably; sanctions for doing so render such actions self-destructive (see, for example, equitable subordination, below). Rather, careful and justified action that is clearly permitted under the agreement between the parties is perfectly appropriate, and it may even force the debtor's hand on the question of voluntary bankruptcy. This may or may not be what the claimant is seeking, so bear in mind that this may be the result of any enforcement actions against the debtor. But observe that this is one means of addressing the problem of delayed filing, as discussed above.

Thus far, we have considered the filing decision and its effects. Of course, bankruptcy deals ultimately with the debtor's property and its disposition. But what property are we talking about, and who has claims or interests in it? Whose claims are more important? And are there any rights enjoyed by the debtor, or are the creditor's rights the only material interest of the bankruptcy proceeding? These issues are considered in the following chapter.

CHAPTER 3

The Estate

Claims, Priorities, and Interests in Property

Having filed a bankruptcy petition, the debtor's property becomes the central focus of the proceedings. As we discussed above, the date of the petition establishes a demarcation point between pre-petition and post-petition events and interests. This means that there are two issues with which to be concerned: First, the identity of the parties and the nature of their interests in the pre-petition property of the debtor, and second, the post-petition maintenance, use, and disposition of the property. Figure 1.1 provides a schematic overview of the relationship between the automatic stay and the property issues discussed in this chapter. Note that upon filing, both the automatic stay and the creation of the estate occur automatically and immediately. The reader is encouraged to refer again to the stay provisions discussed in Section 2.1.5.2, and also should bear in mind that claimants may seek relief from the stay (or adequate protection) to monetize or protect their interest in any property included in the estate. To that extent, the stay and the nature of the estate are interconnected, so the dichotomy depicted in Figure 1.1 should not be read as absolute.

3.1 Creation and Composition of the Estate

When the debtor files its bankruptcy petition, its property is no longer subject to its sole interest and discretion. In bankruptcy parlance, the filing creates an "estate" that is to be managed and administered for the benefit of all claimants, subject to their individual rights and entitlements.[1] In effect, then, the estate is a different legal entity from the pre-petition debtor. The pre-petition rights of claimants in the debtor's property are fixed as of the date of filing, and subsequent decisions concerning the property's use or disposition, or a particular claimant's ability to act against the collateral, are made in light of the value of the property to the estate and the joint interests of all claimants. As we will see shortly, not all claimants enjoy the same rights and interests; some are, recalling Orwell, more equal than others. But unlike pre-petition relationships, where the debtor can dispose of its property virtually at will, or where a secured creditor can execute on its security interest without regard to the position of other creditors (at least those junior to its interest), neither the debtor nor an individual claimant, secured or not, has unconditional rights in the property of the debtor in the post-petition environment. The estate thus represents a bundle of interests in property, theoretically all of which are to be considered in determining allowable rights to use, sell, leverage, or secure.

Battlegrounds

1. Inclusion of property in the estate: Questions of fact may arise concerning the nature of the debtor's interest that may permit exclusion. Such exclusions, however, are relatively unusual. See 3.1.1.

2. Post-petition rights: It may be possible for interests in property to be distinguished as belonging to the debtor rather than to the estate. The same technical distinction, though, may limit other rights, as where interests in debtor property do not automatically transfer to property of the estate. See 3.1.2 and 3.1.3.

3. Claim subordination: Existing claims may be subject to subordination to others, for example in cases where abuse may be provable, or creditors may adjust priorities by negotiation. Debtors may thus seek new financing conditioned upon completion of such an agreement between the creditors, a situation that may confer leverage to various parties depending on the facts of the case. See 3.2.4.

4. Valuation: Property value is a critical, and highly contentious issue that affects not only the amount of the expected distribution but also priority status of the claimants. See 3.2.5.1 and 3.2.5.2.

5. Debtor in possession financing: Post-petition credit extended to the debtor organization is given priority status, and thus may alter existing priorities and the likelihood of those claimants' recoveries. See 3.2.5.3.

6. Preferential transfers: Certain pre-petition transfers of property may be voidable in bankruptcy. See 3.3.2.2; also see 3.3.2.4, avoidance of transfers deemed fraudulent.

3.1.1 *Property of the Estate*

The Code provides a broad, generalized description of property that becomes part of the estate upon filing. All "legal and equitable interests" in property are included, meaning not only direct title but also any beneficial interests in property (usually something that concerns only individual debtors, as in the case of a trust beneficiary).[2] The nature of legal interest is such that ownership and non-ownership interests are included; thus, the debtor's interests as a lessee are part of the estate, as are any unsatisfied claims of the debtor against other parties, whether under contract (breach of contract actions, for example) or law (claims that might be brought against others for negligent conduct, including actions against directors and officers of the debtor). And the property may be "under the sole, equal, or joint management and control of the debtor."[3] Accordingly, any joint interest of the debtor in property becomes part of the estate, even if the other joint interests are not debtors in the case.

Individual debtors are permitted exemptions of personal property under applicable state law (recall some of the historical precedents of these allowances from Chapter 1), but in general the property and interests of corporate debtors are subject to inclusion in the estate regardless of form or content. The Code excludes from the estate "any power that the debtor may exercise solely for the benefit of an entity other than the debtor,"[4] and interests of the debtor as a lessee of commercial property under leases expiring prior to or during the bankruptcy proceedings.[5] Obviously, these exceptions to the general rule of inclusion are very limited in scope, so the important thing to remember is that virtually any property interest of any kind existing as of the filing date becomes property of the estate.

At this point, we need also to consider the issue of property rights themselves. In other words, if we say that in most cases all property of the debtor becomes property of the estate, what gives rise to the property interest in the first place? Note that this is actually a different question from that animating the determination of what becomes property of the estate. The latter question is based on which of the debtor's property interests come into the bankruptcy proceedings. Here, we are asking how those property interests actually are identified. Obviously, legal ownership will be the most common form of property interest encountered, and there is little room for debate in most cases. But even in such cases, questions concerning the validity of title may be encountered. Matters such as these ultimately must be determined under state law governing ownership rights and interests. Thus, if state law gives the debtor an ownership or property interest, then in most circumstances that interest becomes property of the bankruptcy estate.

A corollary consideration is the treatment of property transfers, or more pertinently limitations on transfers. This is relevant because, as a technical matter, to say that property of the debtor becomes property of the estate implies a transfer of interest from one to the other. Again, remember that we are dealing with a different legal creature from the pre-petition debtor when we consider the estate. The problem that can be encountered is that contracts or agreements of the debtor may limit its right to transfer the subject property to other parties, as may regulations or other rules to which the debtor or its business is subject. The general rule under the Code is that property of the debtor becomes property of the estate notwithstanding any limitation on transfer or the grant of a right to foreclose or terminate based on the debtor's financial insolvency or the act of filing a bankruptcy petition.[6] Thus, if I lease equipment to you for use in your business, and include in our agreement a limitation on your right to transfer the property, that limitation does not survive bankruptcy or operate against the estate. Likewise, if I include a clause giving me the right to repossess the equipment if you become insolvent or file bankruptcy, but you file before I am able to exercise my rights in the property, I cannot enforce the agreement and your property interest enters into the estate. I am then simply a claimant in your bankruptcy case. Season tickets, arguably a license and usually stipulated as non-transferable by the selling team, also have been found to be property of the estate and subject to sale in bankruptcy.[7]

Assuming a final determination of the debtor's property is made for purposes of defining the interests of the estate, there remains the not uncommon case of a debtor corporation doing business in multiple states, and perhaps nationally. The Code provides that property interests become part of the estate "wherever located and by whomever held."[8] Moreover, property of the debtor in the hands of others must be returned to the estate for administration during the pendency of the bankruptcy.[9] Thus, the debtor cannot "hide" assets by attempting to elude direct jurisdiction of the court, and anyone holding property of the debtor is under an affirmative obligation to surrender it to the estate. Debtors with property in multiple jurisdictions retain their property interests, all of which become property of a single bankrupt estate upon filing.

3.1.2 Post-petition Property Rights

Having looked at the question of the debtor's pre-petition property and the nature and composition of the estate, we need also to look at the handling of property acquired *after* the petition. As a general rule, the estate automatically includes any property acquired by the estate after the filing, together with "proceeds, product, offspring, rents, or profits of or from property of the estate."[10] Here we have a potential complication: Note that the language used refers to the estate and to property of the estate. As a result, an interested party might be able to challenge a determination of inclusion by separating the interests of the debtor from those of the estate, or establishing a distinction between profits earned from estate property and those earned from property excluded from the estate. For example, if a claim wholly unrelated to any pre-petition property arises after the bankruptcy filing, or if property actually excluded from the estate were to be sold, any proceeds ultimately realized could be characterized as belonging to the debtor, and not to the estate. Thus, sometimes the facts allow this kind of separation of interests, and it is important to be aware of the potential for such distinctions to be raised.

Another key issue in the consideration of post-petition interests concerns the treatment of security interests. It is very common to observe what is known as an after-acquired property clause in a security agreement, which gives the creditor a continuing security interest in all property of the kind covered by the agreement that the debtor owns at present or in the future. Let us assume that Lender extends a working capital loan to Deadbeat, Inc., secured by Deadbeat's furniture, fixtures, and equipment (FF&E), and that the language of the security agreement covers "all furniture, fixtures and equipment now owned or acquired hereafter." Proper steps are taken to perfect the security interest (see Section 3.2 below). Deadbeat defaults on the obligation and, immediately prior to Lender's execution against the collateral, files bankruptcy.

Clearly, Deadbeat's FF&E represent a property interest that will become part of the estate. And equally clearly, Lender has a secured claim against Deadbeat's *pre-petition* FF&E. The question, though, is whether Lender's security interest extends to any FF&E acquired by Deadbeat following the bankruptcy petition. Outside of bankruptcy it would, but the Code provides that "property acquired by the estate or by the debtor after the commencement of the case is not subject to any lien resulting from any security agreement entered into by the debtor before the commencement of the case."[11] Newly acquired FF&E will be subject only to any new security agreement entered into in connection with its purchase. The only exception to this rule concerns the case in which the creditor has a security interest in the proceeds or profits of the property subject to the security interest. Thus, in our example, while the post-petition FF&E would not be subject to Lender's security interest, if Deadbeat were to sell the pre-petition property (subject to court approval in the bankruptcy proceedings), Lender's claim would attach to the proceeds of the sale.

3.1.3 Abandonment

The final consideration worthy of mention here relates to property that initially is part of the estate but which subsequently comes to be viewed as unimportant to the administration of the bankruptcy. In such cases, it is possible to abandon the property. Following a hearing on the matter, "property of the estate that is burdensome to the estate or that is of inconsequential value and benefit to the estate" may be abandoned.[12] The effect of this determination, of course, is to relinquish the estate's interest in that property and to return it to the debtor for disposition outside of the bankruptcy proceedings. Note that this may facilitate the kind of debtor/estate distinctions mentioned above with respect to the question of post-petition interests and earnings. In general, though, courts are likely to permit abandonment only when the property in question truly is worthless (an outdated plant sitting on a toxic waste site, for example) or when the property is fully encumbered and thus abandoned to the creditor for satisfaction of its lien interest. But again, it is important to be aware of the possibility of abandonment and to understand its implications.

3.2 Claims and Priorities

3.2.1 Establishing Claims

Once a case is commenced and the debtor has scheduled its existing obligations, the burden shifts to creditors and other claimants to establish the nature of their claims. In a Chapter 7 case, all unsecured claimants must file a proof of claim with the court within 90 days of the meeting of creditors in order to substantiate their interests in the bankruptcy estate.[13] The proof of claim requires not just a statement of the obligation, but also must be supported by the original document under which the obligation arose. In Chapter 11 proceedings, the debtor's schedule of obligations is considered prima facie evidence of the validity of the creditor's claims, and proofs of claim are not necessary unless the creditor or claimant was not scheduled by the debtor or there is some dispute about the nature or amount of the obligation.[14] All such claims then are deemed allowed, unless the debtor or another claimant objects, in which case a hearing will be held and the court will enter an order specifying the amount of the claim allowed.

3.2.2 Attachment and Perfection

In order to establish the rights of claimants in a bankruptcy proceeding, the nature of their claims must be identified and ranked. It is commonplace to speak of such rankings as the order of liquidation and to speak of equity owners as the holders of a residual claim that is satisfied after payment of all other debts. This is true as a general matter, but glosses over the stratification of debt and other claims against the debtor. Even more sophisticated statements of priority that recognize the distinction between secured and unsecured indebtedness still are overly general given the existence under the Code of different classifications within each of these categories. These distinctions are important even for secured creditors to understand, for they can affect strategies and approaches to both pre- and post-petition decisions.

Before we look at the order of priorities, we need to return to the basics of lending practice and the creation of liens that are secured by collateral. Initially, remember that the distinction between secured and unsecured claims is just this: In the former, collateral underlies the debt, while no collateral supports the latter. When a debt obligation intended to be secured by collateral is created, there must be an agreement signed by the debtor granting to the creditor a security interest in specific collateral. This is sufficient to create an interest in the collateral that is binding upon the debtor, and we generally say that *attachment* has occurred at this point. However, attachment alone is insufficient. The claim is not secured until it is perfected, which asserts the rights of the creditor *against other potential creditors and claimants.* In other words, absent perfection, the debtor can continue to pledge the same collateral over and over, and while each creditor will possess a valid and enforceable debt obligation, the collateral interest of the creditors will become weaker and weaker as the process continues, given that recovery from a liquidation of the collateral would have to be spread across the multiplicity of debts.

So perfection is necessary to create and obtain the status of a secured creditor. As noted above in "Terminology," the method of perfection will vary by state and by the type of collateral involved, so that it will be necessary to be fully conversant with the procedures and requirements that apply in a given state to the specific collateral in question. And this raises another important policy observation about the Code: The specific intent of the Code was to build upon state law in such a way that the rights of the parties to a bankruptcy are a function of state law that then carry over into federal bankruptcy law and procedure, creating something of a hybrid legal regime.

Now consider the question of interstate transactions. Suppose that Creditor is headquartered in State A, while Debtor does business in States A, B, and C, and has property in all three. Where do we perfect if we are Creditor? The facts of a case and the nature of the collateral involved will shape the decision, and perhaps might even limit our options, but if we are Creditor, in most cases it would be wise to perfect in all three states, especially if the collateral is something that might be moved from state to state or is fungible. Again, the idea is to provide notice to other potential creditors that Creditor has an interest in this type of collateral. Since Debtor does business in three states, it is reasonable to assume that it might seek financing in any or all, and that that financing might entail a pledge of similar collateral. On the other hand, if the collateral is real property, then recording the mortgage or deed of trust against the specific property in the county in which it is located is sufficient.

3.2.3 Effect of Perfection

As we have seen, perfection gives notice to potential creditors of our interest in specific collateral. Perfection thus validates and protects our interest not only against a debtor, but also against third parties. This doesn't necessarily mean that our borrower or other creditors can't act or transact with respect to that collateral. Returning to our example above, assume we have perfected our interest in specific collateral (by perfecting in all states in which Debtor does business) but Debtor nevertheless enters into a subsequent security agreement with a small Australian bank, Down Under Depository (or "DUD" for short), that is unfamiliar with American practice. In this case, DUD doesn't search the public records to determine whether or not a pre-existing lien exists against the collateral offered by Debtor. DUD extends the loan, but does perfect its own interest in the collateral. Debtor later defaults and files a bankruptcy petition. Leaving aside the potential intricacies of international practice for the moment, clearly under American law both Creditor and DUD have an interest in the same collateral, and both have perfected against that collateral. It might seem unethical for Debtor to have pledged the same collateral twice, and perhaps Debtor even intended to deceive DUD in this way, knowing or suspecting that a foreign lender might be unaware of domestic legal requirements. Notwithstanding such considerations, there is no law that automatically prohibits this kind of activity, the potential fraud being a separate issue. *With both creditors having an interest in the same collateral, the determination of rank is based upon prior perfection.* Thus, Creditor wins and is accorded the higher priority, and DUD stands second in line with respect to the collateral, assuming there is anything left after satisfying Creditor's claim. Its lack of knowledge of Creditor's security interest is immaterial to its own rights in the collateral. To state simply: the principle of first in time applies to situations such as this.

3.2.4 Subordination of Claims

Assume now that Debtor had no fraudulent or unethical intentions, and naturally assumed that its new lender, DUD, would follow common financial practice and discover the pre-existing lien. What are DUD's options if, in fact, it discovered Creditor's lien following a search of the public records, or Debtor is completely forthcoming and discloses the existence of the lien to DUD? Obviously, DUD can accept the transaction as it stands and assume an inferior position to Creditor. Perhaps, knowing the situation, DUD can negotiate different terms on the loan with Creditor, possibly including a higher-than-normal interest rate or some other form of compensation for its inferior security status, and perhaps this is perfectly acceptable. Many lenders extend credit and accept collateral on an "abundance of caution" basis. There are obvious dangers to this practice, but if some other form of compensation is offered or required it may be deemed an acceptable risk, particularly if the borrower is considered reliable or a longstanding relationship exists between the lender and the borrower.

But another option would be to approach Creditor and seek to negotiate an intercreditor agreement or even a subordination agreement. In the case of the former, the intercreditor agreement would specify the distribution of proceeds of the collateral between the competing lenders. A subordination agreement would, on these facts, explicitly subordinate Creditor's interests to those of DUD, notwithstanding the subsequent perfection. Creditor might accept such an offer if some compensation were offered, perhaps in the form of a principal reduction by Debtor, or the posting of additional collateral. Or perhaps it would be a matter of prudent negotiation: Debtor tells Creditor it will be forced to default without DUD's loan, and DUD will not extend the new loan without either an intercreditor or subordination agreement. Perhaps Creditor has some doubt as to whether the existing collateral will be sufficient to cover its loan, or, in the converse, knows that the collateral is more than sufficient to cover both loans, and therefore acquiesces on the assumption that the new financing will allow Debtor to avoid default in any case and regain its financial footing. Many other similar scenarios might develop. If a creditor desired to avoid the prospect of such contingencies, it could stipulate that any such subsequent pledge of the collateral by the borrower, without approval of the creditor, would constitute default under the terms of their agreement. Banks frequently insert such clauses in their loan agreements, but it is something for other creditors to bear in mind as well.

Now assume the parties in our scenario reached an agreement, but Debtor still ended up in bankruptcy court. Such agreements are explicitly enforceable in bankruptcy.[15] Thus, as long as the agreement is valid under the governing state's body of contract law, it will be enforceable in bankruptcy. Although we have considered the matter in terms of two secured creditors, the principle can be extended to claimants of any type who desire to alter their standing in a potential bankruptcy. Two unsecured creditors might, for example, alter their priority status, as when a senior unsecured creditor agrees to subordinate its claim to a junior unsecured creditor.

Complications in this kind of arrangement are common where other intervening claimants exist. This can be illustrated as follows: You are standing in line to purchase a ticket at a movie theater (perhaps for the first screening of the year's hottest movie or the inevitable Star Wars reprise). You know the theater is getting full and that some in line might not get in, but based on your rough count of those already in and those ahead of you, you are reasonably certain that you're in good shape. Suddenly, Claim Jumper walks up from somewhere in the back of the line, gets in line just in front of you with someone he knows, and ends up buying the last available ticket. Translated back to a business setting, this shows us that our position in a distribution or liquidation may not be what we think it is if it happens that a claimant inferior to us has a subordination agreement with a superior claimant; while we may think that we are in line to receive some benefit, another claimant might jump in front of us in the priority list and be entitled to distribution (perhaps the final one at that). Remember, too, that these subordination agreements may not be made public, particularly if we are dealing with unsecured creditors, and that these are pre-petition agreements that are not subject to court and general claimant approval. Thus, it is important, where practicable, to have some understanding in your agreement with the debtor regarding the periodic disclosure of existing obligations. Banks, again, tend to do something like this frequently, but others may wish to follow suit. If nothing else, doing so will help you assess the debt coverage prospects of the debtor, but it may also help you identify existing intercreditor arrangements, or open doors to you for your own agreement, prior to bankruptcy. Debtors may or may not have an interest in such matters, but may be able to negotiate favorable outcomes in exchange for assistance, at least where not required to cooperate by circumstance or contract.

There is one more complication in the story of subordination that is worthy of note at this juncture. The Code also empowers the court to impose an "equitable subordination" of interests where necessary to benefit the estate.[16] Equitable subordination is a common law concept arising from the historical split between courts of law and courts of equity. As the name suggests, the purpose of the doctrine is to ensure fairness and justice, and therefore it should come as no surprise that the most obvious application of equitable subordination arises in cases of dishonesty or abuse. Lender liability claims, for example, often give rise to equitable subordination of that creditor's interest. But other, less egregious bases may be asserted as well. There have been applications of the doctrine made in leveraged buyout cases, where the structure of the original transaction was deemed unduly harmful to non-participant claimants.[17] Similarly, one would expect that private equity transactions, many of which involve payment of fees in addition to the assumption of significant debt obligations, could be viewed in the same light. Other transactions in which ownership might be arranged to appear as a debt transaction, thereby according a higher priority in liquidation, also might run afoul of the doctrine.

Thus, care should be taken in the structure of any transaction, with an understanding that today's advantageous provisions may be tomorrow's subordination in a bankruptcy proceeding. The Code does not limit the court's authority in this respect; matters that come before the court on equitable subordination grounds will be subject to a "smell test" that may depend greatly upon an individual judge's appraisal of the facts. On a more positive note, it is true that the court is not permitted to simply issue an order for subordination because of a feeling that one creditor is somehow more deserving than another, or because of general preferences; there must be some basis in fact and law for such a finding. But there is no black letter law on the subject that clearly delineates which actions or transaction structures are acceptable and which are not, and thus it is important to keep this principle in mind when dealing with a debtor either prior to or during a bankruptcy proceeding.

3.2.5 Priorities

Having dealt with the creation and practical effects of claims and priorities, we will turn now to an examination of the actual priorities that govern bankruptcy distribution, whether in Chapter 7 or Chapter 11.

It is important to recall the principle of absolute priority at this juncture. In its strictest meaning, the doctrine requires payment in full of a claim *before* the next claimant in order of priority receives even partial satisfaction of the amount owed. This is why priorities matter, particularly when the value of the estate may not be sufficient to pay all claimants in full. As we will see later, in Chapter 11 cases absolute priority may or may not hold in this strict sense, but it is the organizing principle that animates and shapes the process.

3.2.5.1 Secured Claims

Table 3.1 sets forth the order of claim priorities. Topping the list, as we have suggested previously and as is generally well known, are secured claims. Interestingly, though, nothing in the Code itself explicitly accords

Table 3.1. Order of Priorities in Bankruptcy

I. Secured claims (506(a)(1))
   a. Fully secured: Collateral value equal to or greater than amount of claim; claimant entitled to amount of claim plus post-petition interest, fees, and costs (506(b)).
   b. Undersecured: Collateral value less than amount of claim. Considered secured as to portion of claim covered by collateral value, and unsecured as to remainder. No entitlement to interest, fees, and costs.

II. Priority claims (unsecured) (507)
   a. Domestic support obligations
   b. Administrative expenses associated with preservation and operation of estate
      i. Superpriority claims: post-petition financing (364) or adequate protection compensation (507(b))
      ii. General administrative expenses, including post-petition financing
   c. Claims arising in ordinary course of business in involuntary cases between time of petition time of acceptance by court
   d. Wages and salaries within 180 days before filing (limited amount)
   e. Contributions to employee benefit plans (limited amount)
   f. Farmer/fisherman claims against storage or processing debtors (limited amount)
   g. Individual claimants for pre-petition deposits on property or services not delivered
   h. Various governmental tax claims
   i. Claims for capital maintenance of insured banks
   j. Personal injury/death claims related to auto/boat accidents attributable to intoxication

III. General unsecured claims

IV. Equity

this priority to secured claims. One must infer this result from the structure of the Code, which treats secured and unsecured claims in separate sections (Sections 506 and 507, respectively). Also supporting the notion is Section 361's requirement for adequate protection of secured claims (and the lack of anything similar for unsecured claims). But the central foundation for the principle actually can be found in general corporate law, which is imported into the Code and bankruptcy process as an enforceable non-bankruptcy right or interest. Here again we see the Code as an overlay to other bodies of law.

What is also less well understood is the Code's distinction between fully secured (referred to as oversecured) and undersecured claims. Suppose that a creditor is owed $10 million and obtains a security interest. At the time the debtor files a bankruptcy petition, the collateral securing the $10 million obligation is worth $10.1 million. The creditor is fully secured, and thus entitled to post-petition interest, fees, and costs. Suppose the case continues for longer than expected, and interest continues to accrue at the contract rate of 5%. On these facts, the creditor would be entitled to only an additional $100,000 of such interest, fees and costs, even though $500,000 in interest would accrue in the first year. The creditor's claim is limited by the value of the collateral in excess of the original obligation.[18] Note also that the accrual rate in this example is based on the contract rate; in general, this is the safest course of action for a creditor to pursue.[19]

Suppose now that the property securing our creditor's claim is worth only $9 million. Under the Code's treatment, the creditor's claim is bifurcated between a secured portion of $9 million, representing the value of the collateral, and an unsecured portion of $1 million. The creditor then would proceed to pursue both claims, and would be entitled to settlement for each based upon the separate status of each claim (i.e., secured in one instance, unsecured in the other). Depending on the case, this obviously might entail a complete loss of the unsecured claim. And perhaps more importantly, the creditor in this situation is *not* entitled to post-petition interest.

3.2.5.2 Valuation

One other issue that the reader may have considered as we discussed the foregoing scenarios is the determination of collateral value. The Code provides that "such value shall be determined in light of the purpose of the valuation and of the proposed disposition or use of such property."[20] This would seem to suggest that a distinction between a liquidation value and a normal use value based on some market price could exist. Note that either could be argued for in a given case, but that even if we agree on the general valuation approach to be used, the actual calculation of value can be disputed with ease.

The importance of valuation cannot be understated. Valuation will affect a secured creditor's status as either oversecured or undersecured, for example, as we discussed in the preceding section. But there are also issues involving the rate of depreciation, which could affect a creditor's right to seek relief from the stay or to seek adequate protection (see Section 2.1.5.2). On these matters, the debtor might be inclined to dispute the valuation, perhaps even to seek to assess a higher value so as to retain possession of the collateral or reduce any adequate protection payments. Other claimants might also seek to challenge valuations, especially if doing so converted an oversecured claim to an undersecured claim or served to minimize interest accrual. Valuation thus is both critical and controversial—and opens the door to a variety of strategic plays by all parties involved.

3.2.5.3 Other Priorities, Administrative Expenses, and Superpriorities

The balance of the priorities itemized by Table 3.1 shows another division among the unsecured claims, specifically between priority claims and general unsecured claims. A cursory review of the list of priority claims will reveal that, for the most part, they are limited in scope and/or amount, arising in many cases in specific circumstances that are not applicable to all bankruptcies. All were placed in the Code for varying policy reasons, but for the moment it is sufficient to observe that these priority claims will reduce the value of the general unsecured creditors' claims precisely because they are accorded priority in distribution. But again, amounts due under these categories are likely to be relatively small in most cases, and in the case of domestic support obligations, will not apply at all to corporate bankruptcy cases, at least outside of claims arising in family business bankruptcies whose owners simultaneously are engaged in this kind of domestic litigation.

The exception to this general observation relates to the administrative expenses priority. These are expenses incurred post-petition for the purpose of administering or preserving the estate, and are accorded priority as an incentive to undertake such activities as will benefit all claimants in the proceedings. And given the receipt of this benefit, the theory underlying the provision is that the claimants should, in effect, pay those expenses out of their recovery. Note, however, that this simply reduces the pool of assets available for distribution in the first place.

The more specific issue with which to be concerned relates to the items labeled in Table 3.1 as superpriorities. Liens or other interests granted to compensate a claimant lacking adequate protection are accorded this higher right of distribution (see also Section 2.1.5.2).[21] If the claimant succeeds in obtaining an order for adequate protection of its interest in the collateral, but subsequently discovers that the extra payment or lien granted in accordance with the order is insufficient (for example, if the property is permitted to be sold at a later date but sells for much less than anticipated), the deficiency (in our example, the difference between the selling price and the amount of the claim) is accorded superpriority status over any other administrative expenses.

Equally important is the priority accorded post-petition financing. Referred to as DIP financing (for "debtor in possession"), the Code grants special privileges to post-petition creditors.[22] The rationale for this provision is that, particularly when we are concerned with the rehabilitation of the debtor organization, we must have equal concern for its ability to maintain adequate cash flow, including additional credit. But if additional credit is needed, what lender would provide it when the prospective borrower is in bankruptcy and other creditors already are lining up for settlement? Hence, in order to square the circle, the Code arranged an incentive, granting priority, and even superpriority claims, to creditors assuming the risk of lending in bankruptcy.

Under the Code, there are four different kinds of DIP financing available, with corresponding differences in procedure and priority:

- Unsecured credit arranged in the ordinary course of business receives priority as an administrative expense;
- After a hearing, other unsecured credit may be permitted, and receives priority as an administrative expense;

- If unsecured credit cannot be obtained under the above conditions as an administrative expense, then, after a hearing, the court may authorize obtaining credit:
  1. With a superpriority over all general administrative claims;
  2. Secured by a lien on property not otherwise subject to a lien; or
  3. Secured by a junior lien on property already subject to a lien.
- After a hearing, the court may allow credit secured by an equal or senior lien on property already subject to a lien if:
  1. Credit is unavailable otherwise; and
  2. There is adequate protection of any creditor's existing claim against the property subject to the new lien (and the burden of proof lies with the debtor in this instance).

Several observations need to be made about this list. First, note that the ordinary-course financing allowance is a matter of right under most circumstances; a hearing is not a prerequisite, as it is under the other provisions. Typically, we are speaking of so-called trade credit here, but the provision is broad enough to encompass other arrangements as well. What this means for claimants is that unless an objection to the debtor's financing plans can be sustained, the debtor is permitted to operate its business and obtain routine credit. And it may be important at least for unsecured claimants to challenge such financing because, although ordinary-course financing is intended to be unsecured, the priority status awarded as an administrative expense means that the creditors extending the financing are paid prior to other existing general unsecured claimants. The key in most cases likely would entail a challenge to the ordinary-course status of the new financing, specifically by asserting that the credit is not, in fact, routine under the normal operations of the debtor. Obviously, this will be fact specific, but both debtors and claimants need to understand the allowance in terms of the debtor's "ordinary course of business." Persuading a court of the merits of a challenge also may be difficult given the permissiveness of the ordinary-course allowance and the possible consequences that might follow the abrogation of any credit arrangements undertaken by the debtor.

The second form of DIP financing can be characterized as non-ordinary-course credit. Note that this requires a hearing as a prerequisite. Successful challenges to ordinary-course financing may end up in this category, as would any clearly extraordinary arrangements initiated by the debtor that cannot reasonably fit within the notion of "ordinary course of business." Unlike the ordinary-course financing considered above, challenges here would have to be based upon the necessity or terms of the financing. Allowed credit under this provision again receives priority treatment as an administrative expense of the estate, payable before general unsecured claims.

From the standpoint of claimants, the hard cases arise in the third and fourth categories, both of which at least require hearings prior to the allowance of the financing. It is here that we observe the potential superpriority of the new claim or the granting of a new lien, which of course confers secured status. To begin with the third category, we should observe that there are actually two different possible outcomes contemplated by the statute. One is the allowance of unsecured credit with a superpriority claim, which represents the difference between this form of financing and the preceding two types. In other words, if the debtor cannot obtain credit on any other terms, the court may permit the financing with a superpriority claim (not just an administrative expense priority as we were contemplating above). We can think of this provision as something of an incentive to ensure the acquisition of sufficient credit when creditors otherwise still would be concerned about lending, even if granted the normal administrative expense priority. Note that this sets up an interesting game among potential DIP creditors (and the debtor in its negotiations with them): Do I hold out for the superpriority, knowing that if any other creditor lends to the debtor without that condition, I lose the business? The nature of this game obviously will change on a case-by-case basis, particularly with respect to the condition of the debtor and the number of available and interested potential DIP lenders, but the existence of the incentive and the nature of negotiations given that incentive should not be overlooked.

But let us now assume that this is still not enough to entice DIP lenders. The second option available to the court is to allow the financing, but also to grant a security interest in otherwise unencumbered property or a junior lien on property already subject to a security interest. Again, in either case less property is available to general unsecured claimants, and the elevation to secured status provides an even greater priority to the new lenders than the superpriority would (remember, the superpriority is still representative of an unsecured claim). This is an issue with which even secured creditors might be concerned, for the encumbrance of additional property may diminish the success of their own adequate protection motions by making less property available to them for that purpose. Even the junior lien provision does not completely ameliorate this concern: Granted, the existing secured creditor is entitled to priority against the collateral, but its "equity" cushion in the collateral still is diminished, and if the existing secured creditor were to succeed in convincing the court to permit the liquidation of the collateral (as not essential to the reorganization, per above), it would have to proceed cautiously in that liquidation. The position of the junior claimant would permit it to challenge the validity of the sale and especially the adequacy of the sale procedures and the valuation of the collateral. The junior claimant, in other words, could assert that the senior creditor did not properly conduct the liquidation, settled for too little, or otherwise failed to maximize the recovery.

The fourth category,[23] which involves the grant of an equal or senior lien in encumbered collateral, should be even more troubling for most secured creditors. Consider: Pre-petition, you required collateral as a condition of extending a loan, and you perfected your interest in the collateral in order to obtain secured creditor status and priority. The debtor defaults and enters bankruptcy. Your position seems unassailable, but suddenly the court grants a new creditor a lien equal to or superior to your own in *your* collateral. You are now relegated to a lower and less privileged status than you thought you were entitled to upon entering bankruptcy. Even in the case of an equal priority lien, your chances of receiving the same distribution you counted upon as the holder of the sole interest in that collateral probably have diminished, and, as discussed above, you may even be undersecured as a result of the new lien.

Options available to the claimant in such cases may be limited. But for those who might want to prevent the lien from being granted, note that the statute provides for satisfaction of two conditions precedent, either of which can be challenged in court. First, the debtor must be unable to obtain financing under any other terms. Whether or not this is true is a question that will be case-specific, and one that sometimes might be akin to proving a negative. But perhaps the debtor rejects arguably better terms because its preferred creditor, based on experience or a long relationship, is offering the less favorable terms. And perhaps these terms result in the subordination of a claimant with whom the debtor happens to have a poor relationship. Maybe this is even the intent of the arrangement. If so, the latter claimant might be able to successfully attack the extension of credit.

Second, the debtor must provide adequate protection of the claimant's interest. As we have seen, proving a lack of adequate protection can be difficult, although the debtor does bear the burden of proof. But this is the more likely line of successful challenge, and may at least result in the provision of extra compensation. And recall that if the extra compensation or collateral proves inadequate, you are entitled to a superpriority over other administrative expenses. Moreover, as we observed in the preceding consideration of junior liens, you might be able to challenge the new creditor's handling of the liquidation process. Still, these observations probably stand as cold comfort given the position the claimant thought it had earned in light of its security interest.

3.3 Use, Disposition, and Recovery of Property

We turn now to consideration of the debtor's own rights in the property of the estate, specifically the right to use, sell, or dispose of such property. We will consider first the basic case of a debtor's ordinary course of business use and disposition of property. Then, in Section 3.3.2, we will consider the issue of avoidance and fraudulent transfers.

3.3.1 Ordinary-course Transactions

Similar to the case of the debtor's obtaining credit in the ordinary course of business, as we discussed above, the Code permits the use, sale, or lease of property in the ordinary course of business.[24] And as we saw in the case of ordinary-course post-petition financing, this right is not dependent upon prior court authorization; no notice or hearing is required as a condition to engaging in any ordinary-course transaction. This will, of course, raise the familiar issue of whether a specific transaction in fact can be construed as "ordinary-course," but subject to challenge after the fact the debtor is free to initiate these kinds of transactions.

There are some limitations on the debtor's right to use property of the estate. First, the debtor cannot use "cash collateral" unless all parties with an interest in that cash collateral consent or the court allows such use following a hearing.[25] "Cash collateral" refers to cash and cash equivalents held by the debtor and in which some party or parties other than the debtor have an interest. Typically, this would arise in conjunction with a lender's security interest in, say, the debtor's accounts receivable and cash equivalents. In the case of the former, as accounts receivable are paid, the cash proceeds become cash collateral in the estate and are subject to the prohibition of use, as would any other cash proceeds of encumbered property sold by the debtor. The significance of this provision is that cash collateral cannot be used by the debtor, even in the ordinary course of business, without authorization from the court or the secured claimants. Note that this may cause cash flow issues for the debtor, and thereby necessitate resort to DIP financing, as discussed above. Given the issues involved in DIP financing and its potential to affect existing priorities, the treatment of cash collateral, including its permissive use, may be a significant negotiating opportunity for both debtor and creditor.

The second limitation on the use of property in the ordinary course of business is represented by the secured claimants' right to challenge the debtor's actions. Secured claimants may seek to block or condition the use or disposition of encumbered property, and the court may so order even without a hearing in order to provide adequate protection of the creditor's interest in the property.[26] This applies not only to property actually used or being used (or sold), but also to property whose use or disposition is *proposed*. The remedy thus is forward looking as well as protective of present interests.

Third, if the debtor is seeking to sell property free and clear of a security interest, which may be the case where a buyer is interested in the property but quite reasonably does not wish to acquire title subject to the original creditor's security interest, the sale may take place only if the creditor so consents, the selling price is greater than the value of all liens against the property, a bona fide dispute exists as to the validity of the creditor's claim, or the creditor could be compelled to accept cash in satisfaction of its claim in other legal proceedings.[27]

Notice that all of these exceptions to the general rule of right-of-use either are very limited in their application or apply only to the interests of secured claimants. Unsecured creditors and other claimants thus have fewer grounds on which to contest the proposed use or sale of property in the ordinary course of business. Indeed, for such claimants, challenging a transaction probably can succeed only on the basis of a challenge to ordinary-course status. This raises an important practical consideration for *purchasers* of estate property: As we will see below, transactions undertaken by the debtor may be avoided by court order. Purchasers thus may wish to seek assurance of the debtor's right to transfer the property in question, whether based on the opinion of counsel or court authorization.

3.3.2 Avoidance Powers and Fraudulent Transfers

In this section, we will consider the treatment of transactions undertaken by the debtor that may be subject to what is known as avoidance, essentially the nullification of the transaction in question. Technically, there are two types of transactions at issue: First, certain *pre-petition* transactions may be avoided and the property reclaimed for the benefit of the estate. Although generally we are concerned with post-petition uses of property in the present discussion, these avoidable transactions affect the composition of the estate and its property interests, and therefore the topic is relevant for consideration in this chapter. There are several different variations on the theme of pre-petition transfers that are subject to avoidance, and we will consider each in turn. Second, we also need to look at certain post-petition transactions that are subject to avoidance. This topic will be considered following our discussion of pre-petition transfers.

3.3.2.1 Avoidance of Pre-petition Transfers

In what is known as the strong-arm clause, the Code permits the avoidance of pre-petition transfers or obligations incurred by the debtor that could be avoided by the assertion of non-bankruptcy law rights.[28]

If, under non-bankruptcy law, the holder of a judicial lien, an unsatisfied execution against the debtor's assets, or a bona fide purchaser of real property *could* void the transaction, the transaction is avoidable *even if such creditors do not actually exist in the case in question.* Typically, this provision arises in cases in which a security interest was taken by a creditor but was not perfected by filing or recording as required by state law for the kind of collateral in question. Where such unperfected interests exist, the hypothetical creditors specified in the statute would be able to avoid the transaction by asserting their superior claims.

In addition, transactions that an *actual* unsecured claimant could avoid under non-bankruptcy law also can be avoided under the strong-arm clause.[29] Cases in which this is true tend to be few in number given the limited powers of unsecured claimants (note the distinction here between secured and unsecured status), and often involve fraudulent transfers that can be attacked as such separately (see below, Section 3.3.2.4). But this provision allows the importation of state law, which may provide extra remedies not available under the Code.[30]

3.3.2.2 Avoidance of Preferential Transfers

Now suppose that one of our previous miscreants, Endrun, Inc., is substantially insolvent, and management suspects that its ultimate destination is bankruptcy. The company, though, is concerned about maintaining its relationships with certain creditors. Fearing that a bankruptcy proceeding might result in a loss for these creditors, Endrun decides to satisfy these preferred creditors. Perhaps there is even a tacit understanding that the creditors will extend new credit once the company emerges from bankruptcy. So, Endrun sells certain assets and pays these creditors in full with the proceeds. Everyone is happy—everyone, that is, but the remaining creditors who must take their chances with recovery in bankruptcy. This is precisely the scenario with which the Code is concerned, and the reason that some transactions of this kind are subject to avoidance. Note again that, outside of bankruptcy, the transactions are perfectly legal; nevertheless, they are impermissible in bankruptcy, representing one of the few instances in which non-bankruptcy law will not be recognized or imported into the bankruptcy proceedings. Recall that as a matter of policy, bankruptcy law seeks a collective resolution that will maximize recoveries for all concerned. The so-called preferential transfers defeat this purpose, and therefore are subject to avoidance.

Note that no blanket statement regarding the invalidity of such transfers has been made. Not all are avoidable, regardless of the nature of the transaction or even the intent of the parties. But at least some will be avoidable and, critically, will be regardless of intent. Under the Code, a transfer is avoidable if it is made:

- to or for the benefit of a creditor;
- in connection with an antecedent debt;
- while the debtor is insolvent;
- within 90 days of the bankruptcy petition, or, in the case of a creditor who can be deemed an insider, within one year of the petition; and
- to enable the creditor to receive more than the creditor would receive in a Chapter 7 liquidation.[31]

We will look at these conditions more closely later in this section. But as an introductory consideration, one of the first questions that should arise upon reviewing this list concerns the definition of "transfer." "Transfer" is defined broadly and includes such acts as the creation of a lien, the retention of title as a security interest, foreclosure, and any method of disposing of property or an interest in property.[32] Thus, payment on an antecedent debt is not the only situation giving rise to an avoidable transfer. In particular, creditors should take note of the inclusion of foreclosures in this definition.

Another definitional question that should be considered early on in the process is the statutory meaning of "insider." Table 3.2 reproduces the relevant components of Section 101(31), the full extent of which includes references to individual debtors and entities other than corporations and partnerships, which are not of immediate concern for purposes of this text. Table 3.3, in turn, provides the full definition of the term "affiliate" from Section 101(2), which is included within Section 101(31)'s general definition of "insider." These definitions are critical to avoidance rights due to the dramatically longer time period for recapture that applies to insider transactions (90 days versus one year).

Table 3.2. Definition of "Insider" (Section 101(31))

The term "insider" includes—
...
(B) if the debtor is a corporation—
(i)   director of the debtor;
(ii) officer of the debtor;
(iii) person in control of the debtor;
(iv) partnership in which the debtor is a general partner;
(v)   general partner of the debtor; or
(vi) relative of a general partner, director, officer, or person in control of the debtor;
(C) if the debtor is a partnership—
(i)   general partner in the debtor;
(ii) relative of a general partner in, general partner of, or person in control of the debtor;
(iii) partnership in which the debtor is a general partner;
(iv) general partner of the debtor; or
(v)   person in control of the debtor;
(E) affiliate, or insider of an affiliate as if such affiliate were the debtor; and
(F) managing agent of the debtor.

Table 3.3. Definition of "Affiliate" (Section 101(2))

The term "affiliate" means—
(A) entity that directly or indirectly owns, controls, or holds with power to vote, 20% or more of the outstanding voting securities of the debtor, other than an entity that holds such securities—
(i)   in a fiduciary or agency capacity without sole discretionary power to vote such securities; or
(ii) solely to secure a debt, if such entity has not in fact exercised such power to vote.
(B) corporation 20% or more of whose outstanding voting securities are directly or indirectly owned, controlled, or held with power to vote, by the debtor, or by an entity that directly or indirectly owns, controls, or holds with power to vote, 20% or more of the outstanding voting securities of the debtor, other than an entity that holds such securities [in one of the two circumstances enumerated in (A)].
(C) person whose business is operated under a lease or operating agreement by a debtor or person substantially all of whose property is operated under an operating agreement with the debtor; or
(D) entity that operates the business or substantially all of the property of the debtor under a lease or operating agreement.

If we are dealing with a statutorily defined transfer, and know which avoidance period applies to the transaction, either the general 90-day window or the longer insider time period, and that the transaction falls within that time, we still must be able to satisfy each of the other elements of listed above in order to avoid the transaction. The first requirement, that the transfer must be one that is made to or for the benefit of a creditor, is another broadly construed provision that applies to more than direct cash payments. Let's return to the case of Endrun, Inc. Suppose that the issue now involves the indebtedness its Eewok subsidiary owes to the commercial lender Dewey, Cheatham, and Howe (DCH). DCH becomes concerned about Eewok's stability and obtains a guarantee of the indebtedness from Endrun in order to bolster its position in an anticipated bankruptcy. Endrun and Eewok subsequently file a bankruptcy petition. The guarantee would be an avoidable transfer, having provided additional benefit to DCH, and DCH would not be permitted to use the guarantee to assert a claim against Endrun's assets.

Likewise, the second element, a transfer related to an antecedent debt, is construed broadly to capture virtually *any* debt arising prior to the transfer in question. We will see shortly that exceptions to the avoidance power cover very short-term gaps between the creation of a debt and the occurrence of a potentially avoidable transfer (perhaps, for example, the delivery service's van breaks down on the way to the courthouse or state agency, creating a delay between the time of the funding of a loan and the physical perfection of the security interest granted by the debtor). But absent such a case, any meaningful difference in the time between the creation of the debt and the transfer will trigger the avoidance power. And it is important to note that the creation date is the relevant metric, not any subsequent payment date or maturity date.

Third, the debtor must have been insolvent at the time of the transfer. "Insolvent" is defined in Section 101(32), which applies the balance sheet test (debts exceeding the fair value of assets, plus, in the case of partnership debtors, each general partner's equity in non-partnership property). Note again that this gives rise to the potential strategic use of valuation as a tool to accomplish one's aim with respect to the transfer.

Finally, the transfer must have resulted in more benefit to the creditor than would be realized in a Chapter 7 liquidation. Thus, in our discussion of Endrun's guarantee of Eewok's indebtedness to DCH, DCH probably would be in position to receive more than it would in a straight liquidation of Eewok's assets given its recourse against Endrun under the guarantee. But suppose now that, instead of the guarantee, DCH forecloses against Eewok's property prior to the bankruptcy filing, and manages to sell the property for its liquidation value. As we mentioned above in connection with the definition of "transfer," foreclosure does give rise to an avoidable transaction. We will discuss this general topic a bit more later in this section, but for now observe that DCH did not improve its position by virtue of the foreclosure (the reason this provision of the Code is referred to as the "improvement-in-position test") and thus would not be subject to avoidance. However, the foreclosure would be avoidable if DCH sold the property for more than its liquidation value.

3.3.2.3 Exceptions to Avoidance of Preferences

As we have just seen, there are specific tests that apply to a determination of avoidance. The Code also provides for several exceptions to the elements of avoidable transfers.[33] If these exceptions apply to the transfer in question, then it is not avoidable even if all of the elements for avoidance are otherwise satisfied. First among these exceptions is the situation in which the parties intended for the transfer to represent a "substantially contemporaneous exchange" for "new value," which the Code defines as "money..., services, or new credit," or the release of previously pledged collateral.[34] This exception thus covers the case of an unavoidable delay in, for example, perfection (as in the delivery van breakdown hypothetical above) that would then constitute a transfer related to an antecedent debt. There is no definition of "substantially contemporaneous exchange," which will be fact-specific and subject to the court's interpretation of the facts and the intent of the parties.

The second exception relates to ordinary course of business transactions.[35] To meet the requirements of this exception, the debt itself must have arisen in the ordinary course of business, and the subsequent transfer must either have been made in the ordinary course of business or "made according to ordinary business terms." The latter provision is intended to incorporate standard market practices, while the former looks at the specific course of dealings followed by the debtor. Thus, in our Endrun hypothetical, if the company made payments to a specific creditor in accordance with the specific terms of the agreements between them, and had done so as a matter of routine practice prior to the bankruptcy, the payments would not be subject to avoidance. However, if Endrun used the proceeds of asset sales to pay specific creditors, and especially to pay them in full prior to the maturity date of the debt, the transfers likely would not fall within this exception.

Third, purchase-money security interests, in other words security interests granted in collateral that the loan actually is used to acquire, are excluded if perfection occurs within 30 days after the debtor acquires the collateral.[36] Note that if perfection does not occur within this time, the act of perfecting the interest would then be considered to arise from an antecedent debt and would be avoidable.

Fourth, if an otherwise avoidable transfer is followed by the extension of some "new value" by the creditor that is unsecured and not paid for or otherwise compensated by another transfer from the debtor, the original transfer is protected to the extent of the new value.[37] This is sometimes referred to as the "net result" rule. The same definition of "new value" we referred to above is used in conjunction with this exception.

The final exception of relevance to us covers so-called floating liens in inventory, receivables, and their proceeds. Floating liens are those in which the secured creditor agrees to make periodic advances over time, each of which is secured by all future collateral of this kind (which, of course, comes and goes in the course of the debtor's business, making specific identification impractical or worthless to the creditor). Theoretically, each such advance falling within the 90-day window (or one year in the case of insiders) could be subject to avoidance. The Code exempts these advances from individual scrutiny by stating that the associated transfers (here represented by the security interest automatically granted in exchange for each advance) are not avoidable, at least to the extent that in the aggregate the advances made during the window period do not reduce the "amount by which the debt...exceeded the [collateral] value" pledged to the secured creditor.[38] What this means is that if the secured creditor holding a floating lien ended up with a reduction in the deficiency owed by the debtor, in other words the amount by which the debt exceeds the collateral value, this would harm the interests of unsecured claimants, who then would have less unencumbered collateral to which to look for satisfaction of their claims. In this instance, the transfers occurring within the window period that reduce this deficiency in favor of the secured creditor would be avoidable.

3.3.2.4 Fraudulent Transfers

Thus far, we have been considering pre-petition transfers that are avoidable under the Code without regard to the actual intent of the debtor. In other words, it is not necessary to prove that the debtor intentionally acted to deceive or defraud any claimant or any other property; all that is necessary is to establish the satisfaction of the requisite conditions for avoidance, without specific proof of the debtor's state of mind. But if we know that, in fact, the debtor acted with intent to deceive or defraud, the Code provides another avoidance remedy.[39] At first glance, this may seem like overkill: Why pursue actual fraud if avoidance can be accomplished on other grounds? Generally speaking, one probably would not do so, but that also explains the importance of the actual fraud remedy, which can give recourse against the debtor and its transferees in situations where the other avoidance provisions do not apply. And one critical distinction is the window of opportunity: In the case of fraudulent transfers, there is a two-year window preceding the bankruptcy, compared to at most one year in the case of preferential transers.[40]

Moreover, avoidance of fraudulent transfers need not *always* establish actual fraud, thus providing the remedy in an even broader array of circumstances. Avoidance can be granted when the debtor makes the transfer "with actual intent to hinder, delay, or defraud," *or* in cases involving "constructive fraud," when the debtor receives "less than a reasonably equivalent value," *and*:

- Was insolvent on the date of transfer or became insolvent as a result;
- Was left with an unreasonably small capital base following the transaction given the nature of its business;
- Intended to incur or believed it would incur debts that could not be repaid as they became due; or

- Made the transfer to an insider, under an employment contract and not in the ordinary course of business.[41]

So, as long as the value received by the debtor in exchange for the transfer is too low, only one of these four conditions needs to be satisfied in order to succeed in avoiding the transaction. Most of the time, either of the first two conditions will be more likely to apply and will be easier to establish. And again, for the sake of emphasis, this is the case even without proof of actual intent to defraud.

Note again the use of the phrase "less than a reasonably equivalent value." As we have seen previously, there is no formal definition or guidance under the Code as to its meaning, and therefore the parties must rely upon controlling case law. Recall our Endrun hypothetical in which its lender, DCH, foreclosed on Endrun's collateral prior to the company's bankruptcy petition. DCH received only the liquidation value of the property. Does this constitute "less than a reasonably equivalent value," when it might be possible to obtain more under normal market conditions? For almost 20 years following the adoption of the Code, courts were split on this question, some finding that liquidation value by definition is less than equivalent value, while others upheld the sale if proper procedures were followed. The U.S. Supreme Court then weighed in on the issue, ruling that a foreclosure conducted in accordance with the requirements of state law results in reasonably equivalent value. Holding otherwise, according to the Court, would invalidate virtually any foreclosure sale, since almost always these are conducted under conditions of some distress that may not yield full market value. And Congress could not have intended this result since the statute uses the language it does instead of a reference to market value.[42] Accordingly, on our facts, DCH's foreclosure is not avoidable. It is important to understand, though, that the Court's holding applies only to foreclosures; other kinds of transactions may not be amenable to the same reasoning, and must be argued on a case-by-case basis.

The two "solvency" conditions also deserve brief discussion. Recall that the Code's definition of solvency incorporates the balance sheet test. Here, the test can be met either before or after the transfer, in the latter case when the loss of the transferred property reduces the debtor's asset valuation. As we have seen before, valuation sometimes is the crux of the problem, but in general this requirement is less difficult to meet than a showing of actual intent. The question of adequate capitalization, though, becomes somewhat murkier, but again will turn on a comparison of the debtor's pre- and post-transfer financial condition.

Assuming we meet the applicable requirements, we can avoid the transfer between the debtor and a third party. This raises a question about that third party's rights. The Code in fact provides a measure of protection to an innocent transferee.[43] If our familiar debtor, Endrun, sells certain assets to a third party, Donuts Under Market (DUM), as part of a turnaround strategy, and is insolvent when it does so, other claimants may have a claim for avoidance if the sales price is less than equivalent value (and as noted above, perhaps even if the transaction nets liquidation value since we are not dealing with a foreclosure). But since DUM paid for the assets, in other words if we are not dealing with a case in which Endrun gave property away, DUM is entitled to a lien or the retention of its interest in the property to the extent of the value given in exchange, as long as it acted in good faith in connection with the transaction. Questions as to a transferee's good faith may arise, though, if the sales price is obviously less than reasonable market value; if I buy a Rolex watch from a street vendor for $200, either the watch is broken or its provenance is uncertain, and I should know better. The actual language of the statute, though, makes this less than clear, for it only requires that the transferee act in good faith and does not impose the commonly encountered condition that the transferee knew or should have known that the transfer was invalid. These are all matters that can be asserted to establish or defend against a motion for avoidance.

3.3.2.5 Post-petition Transfers

Heretofore, we have been concerned with pre-petition transfers undertaken by the debtor. From time to time, questions may arise about the debtor's use or disposition of property in the post-petition environment. The Code permits avoidance of unauthorized post-petition transfers, in other words transfers that neither the Code nor the court has specifically permitted.[44] Recall that the debtor has the right to use, sell, or lease property in the ordinary course of business.[45] If the debtor were to sell property other than in the ordinary course of its business without the court's permission, or if a sale could be characterized as not ordinary-course, a claimant could seek avoidance of the transfer instead of pursuing remedies such as conditioning or prohibiting the sale.[46] In other words, in some cases it might be to a claimant's advantage to allow a transfer to occur and seek avoidance rather than to block the transfer initially. Care must be exercised, of course, since it may be difficult to reclaim the property once it is sold, or its value may decline precipitously in the interim, but the option does exist and may be worth pursuing, especially if the claimant believes the court would only condition the sale anyway. The facts of the specific case will determine which course of action is more practical.

This concludes our consideration of the provisions relevant to general administration of the case. In Chapter 4 we will outline the specific procedures applicable to Chapter 7 liquidations and Chapter 11 reorganizations.

CHAPTER 4

The Mechanics of Chapter 7 and Chapter 11

In Chapters 2 and 3, we looked at the Code's treatment of filing, property of the estate, claims and priorities, and the general administration of a bankruptcy proceeding. It is important to remember that the procedures outlined above apply with equal measure to Chapter 7 and Chapter 11 proceedings, with some distinctions involving liquidations under Chapter 7 that we will touch upon in Section 4.1. This chapter is devoted, instead, to the specific mechanics of liquidations and reorganizations. Figure 1.2 provides a schematic overview of both processes, to which the reader can refer to quickly understand where a given issue stands in relation to others or to the process as a whole.

4.1 Liquidation Under Chapter 7

4.1.1 Filing the Case: Considerations and Implications

As you will recall, Chapter 7 cases may be commenced either voluntarily or involuntarily. In the normal instance of a voluntary petition, we noted that the election of a liquidation proceeding typically is made when the business has no going concern value or its prospects for a successful reorganization, often involving a recapitalization of the business, are minimal. Remember, too, that liquidation cases can be initiated by a conversion from a Chapter 11 filing (see Section 2.1.2 above). Among the more notable liquidation cases of recent years were conversions of Chapter 11 filings by Borders, Circuit City, and Steve & Barry's. All sought recapitalization or the sale of some or all of their businesses, and instead liquidated when the desired outcome did not materialize. It is not uncommon for debtors to enter Chapter 7 in this way, and unfortunately a significant proportion of Chapter 11 filings do so. Liquidations also sometimes follow "successful" reorganizations in which the debtor emerges too weak to compete successfully but with too little asset value to attempt another reorganization.

Battlegrounds

1. Chapter 7 (liquidation)
   - Valuation: Determines precise recovery on liquidation, but subject to the same considerations and problems discussed in Chapter 3. See 4.1.2.
   - Post-petition financing: Available in liquidation cases, as discussed in Chapter 3, and subject to the same issues concerning priorities. See 4.1.2.

2. Chapter 11 (reorganization)
   - Executory contracts: Unfulfilled contracts (including labor agreements) may be assumed or rejected by the debtor, subject to conditions. See 4.2.2.
   - Identification and classification of claims: The debtor initiates the process of plan development by grouping claimants into specific classes. Establishes baseline for negotiations and voting. See 4.2.3.1.
   - Development of plan: Debtor has exclusive right to propose first plan, subject to time limits and other conditions. Rival plans may be offered under certain conditions. See 4.2.3.2 and 4.2.3.3. Valuation remains a critical issue here given its implications for the settlement of claims.
   - Voting and approval: Plan must secure approval of claimants, who vote by class. Holdouts may force renegotiation, but may be subject to cramdown. See 4.2.3.5.

Outcomes of this sort represent a significant waste of asset value and ideally should be avoided. The decision to liquidate a business is hard, of course, but if no realistic prospect of rehabilitation exists it is better to do so sooner rather than later. The subsequent recovery in liquidation almost always is less than might have been realized had the business been liquidated initially, instead of in the aftermath of a failed reorganization. That said, you may recall that I also advised attempting a reorganization first, and it is undoubtedly true that the management teams of Borders, Circuit City, and Steve & Barry's thought they could reorganize successfully and were as surprised as anyone when the necessary financing, purchase agreements, or other contingencies upon which their success hinged were not realized. The point of the present discussion, though, is that, surprises and disappointments aside, some businesses should be liquidated at the first opportunity. This is especially true of those with no going concern value and limited prospects of achieving a successful reorganization. Obviously, there is no magic formula for determining when such criteria are met, but a clear-eyed estimation of the business' prospects should be undertaken prior to bankruptcy; in most cases, an obvious liquidation candidate can be identified, and everyone is better off if that is the choice that is made before asset value is depleted any further.

Unfortunately, as we saw earlier, principally in Section 2.1.4 concerning the question of when to file, such decisions often are delayed for too long given the panoply of incentives and concerns with which the management of distressed firms must grapple. Personal, professional, and psychological factors weigh in the balance of such decisions. Or the debtor may simply postpone the decision, hoping for the best but presiding over a period of extended decline. In addition, the treatment of post-bankruptcy discharges, which we will discuss in more detail below, tends to favor a Chapter 11 filing over liquidation: Specifically, unsatisfied debts are not discharged in liquidations. But while this would seem to be one more reason to attempt reorganization, it is also a reason for true liquidation candidates to tread warily, since if there is no discharge an early liquidation is likely to satisfy more claims than a delayed liquidation.

Notwithstanding these observations, creditors and other claimants should perform their own estimation of recovery value under liquidation or reorganization. If reorganization might yield a better outcome for the claimant, it is important to remember the rules of conversion discussed above in Chapter 2.[1] Generally speaking, in the case of unsecured claimants it is better to make this determination and file the motion to convert early in the proceedings in order to conserve the estate for eventual distribution in a subsequent reorganization. Timing may be a matter of indifference to secured creditors, unless the collateral is likely to deteriorate or lose value. Another consideration for secured creditors is whether their interests are served by conversion at all: As we will see, the mechanics of reorganization may facilitate a redistribution of value from secured creditors to unsecured creditors. Where this can be anticipated, secured creditors obviously would wish to oppose the motion to convert, instead opting to receive the liquidated value of their collateral at the earliest possible date.

The question of whether to choose liquidation or reorganization, then, is obviously a complicated one, and can only be determined by the facts of the specific case. Thus, creditors and other claimants, including even equity holders, should be aware of the issues and incentives of the parties to the case and plan accordingly. At the very least, claimants should respond to a debtor organization's financial distress by increasing their monitoring of the debtor's condition and activities in order to better understand their position in any eventual bankruptcy proceeding and whether to attempt to convert a case. It may be necessary or advisable, given circumstances in a particular case, to impose additional reporting requirements or restrictive covenants that may result in greater leverage. Such monitoring also gives the claimant an opportunity to attempt to improve its position in bankruptcy, perhaps by increasing collateralization or taking collateral for the first time (subject to the rules governing preferential transfers discussed above in Chapter 3). Likewise, management of the debtor organization needs to conduct an objective appraisal of its business and its prospects, as well as the array of claimants in the case and the nature of their interests. Only then can the appropriate determination of whether to liquidate or seek reorganization be made.

But the point of this discussion, and indeed one of the main arguments of this book, is that bankruptcy decisions should be made sooner rather than later. In most cases, delay serves no one's interests. If there is a reasonable prospect of survival and successful reorganization, the debtor probably is better off choosing to reorganize, while if the going concern value of the debtor is in doubt, or if indeed the debtor cannot reasonably be seen to be a going concern at all, it is better to liquidate in the absence of something that suggests reorganization would succeed. In either situation, delay, and the asset depletion that inevitably follows, is everyone's enemy.

4.1.2 Appointment of the Trustee

One of the main distinctions in bankruptcy procedure between liquidations under Chapter 7 and Chapter 11 reorganizations concerns the appointment of a trustee, which is mandatory under Chapter 7. The U.S. Trustee appoints an interim trustee upon the filing of the petition, and the interim trustee serves until a permanent trustee is elected at the meeting of creditors, if a vote is requested by the unsecured creditors. Unsecured creditors without a conflict of interest, such as an insider, then may vote for the permanent trustee.[2] The permanent trustee is deemed elected if a majority of unsecured claims representing 20% of the total of such claims vote in favor. If no candidate satisfies this requirement, as would be true if there were substantial disagreement among the creditors, or if the vote is not requested in the first place, the interim trustee will be appointed to administer the case. As a policy matter, unsecured creditors are given this right to select the trustee in order to provide a measure of protection; secured creditors, of course, will be able to look to their collateral, and in the case of a liquidation we usually are dealing with a very insolvent debtor whose assets may cover very few, if any, of the unsecured claims. Thus, the Code permits these creditors to select the trustee in whom they have the most confidence, since it is this person who will be responsible for the enforcement of their rights.

The primary duty of the trustee, of course, is to "collect and reduce to money the property of the estate," which entails an obligation to maximize the value of the estate, but many other duties, rights, and powers are vested in the trustee by the statute.[3] In particular, the trustee is empowered to enforce rights or obligations arising under the Code, including the right to sue officers or directors for fiduciary breaches, or undertake avoidance actions or make a determination of abandonment, as we discussed in Chapter 3, on behalf of the claimants.

Also at the meeting of creditors, unsecured creditors may vote to elect a committee for purposes of representation. The committee must be comprised of not less than three, nor more than eleven, of the unsecured creditors.[4] The committee then has the right to consult with the trustee and make inquiries or recommendations relating to the administration of the case.

4.1.3 Collection, Liquidation, and Distribution of the Estate

One of the first matters that must be determined following the petition and the election of the trustee is whether or not the debtor will remain in business, and for how long. It is not widely known that liquidations do not always result in immediate, or even near-term, cessation of the debtor's business. The Code authorizes the continuation of the business "for a limited period," under the guidance of the trustee, if the court determines that operation "is in the best interest of the estate and consistent with the orderly liquidation of the estate."[5] This is a factual question that depends upon the specifics of the debtor's business, but in many instances recovery may be facilitated by the debtor's continuation. One such practical example concerns the collection of accounts receivable, which usually would be easier to accomplish under the normal operations of the debtor. More difficult cases may concern operational details, such as the conclusion of pre-petition investment decisions whose outcomes may enhance the value of the estate. In such cases, the trustee may lack the specific knowledge necessary to effectively administer the business in the ordinary course of its dealings. The Code does not provide a definition or offer guidance with respect to the question of how long "a limited period" can or should be, but operations will be allowed to continue only so long as value to the estate can be increased or maximized. All parties should be aware that continuation of the business will not be permitted as a matter of right or for any period of time longer than necessary to collect and "reduce to money" the property of the estate.

By the same token, both the relatively short duration of the case and the limited continuation of the debtor's business effectively condition the exercise of other rights under the Code. Primary among the rights affected in this manner will be the trustee's exercise of the avoidance powers (discussed in Chapter 3) in cases involving preferential or fraudulent transfers. Given the limited time involved in most liquidations, these actions must be undertaken fairly quickly in order to accumulate all possible property for distribution. If the trustee is not aware of the circumstances of pre-petition transfers of property that would give rise to a claim of preferential or fraudulent transfer, the claimants in the case will need to make the trustee aware of the facts at the earliest possible opportunity. This would also apply to potential actions to compel surrender of estate property held by third parties.[6]

The permissive right to obtain unsecured credit in the ordinary course of business[7] also is triggered by the right to operate according to Chapter 7.[8] Unlike a Chapter 11 case, the shorter duration of the typical liquidation case arising from the limited right to operate the business usually means that the opportunities to obtain post-petition financing and grant any new priority claims are limited in comparison to the typical reorganization proceeding. Thus, once a liquidation case is underway, the priorities existing as of the date of the petition often tend to be relatively fixed. But if the debtor is allowed to operate for any length of time, the provision of a superpriority may offer the opportunity of a quick return to a post-petition lender. Claimants once more need to be aware of these mechanisms in estimating their expected recovery and developing liquidation strategies.

Apart from the grant of additional claims in connection with post-petition financing, the trustee has the authority to deal with certain kinds of liens that may result in a slight alteration of the overall priority structure.[9] First, the trustee retains the right to seek equitable subordination of claims.[10] Second, any lien held by a judgment claimant for payment of punitive damages or other similar fines and penalties may be avoided.[11] This avoidance power does not extend, though, to a lien or portion of a lien securing a claim for actual damages. Thus, if the Road Kill Café sells unreasonably hot coffee to a customer who then suffers internal and external burns from sipping and spilling the coffee, and the customer obtains a judgment against Road Kill for actual and punitive damages, any lien securing the judgment for *punitive damages* can be set aside by the Chapter 7 trustee. Any lien securing the judgment for *actual* damages is unaffected. Note also that this avoidance provision applies *only* to the lien, not to the claim itself, which would survive as an unsecured claim.

A measure of good news also can be found in the Code's treatment of tax liens. Tax liens and statutory liens treated as tax liens are subordinated to senior liens on the same property subject to the tax lien, and to holders of priority and administrative claims.[12] Tax liens receive third priority in the subject property, followed by junior lien holders, and then by a deficiency claim owed on the tax lien if proceeds were insufficient to pay the tax lien in full following payment of the two higher priority classes. However, the trustee first must sell all unencumbered property prior to subordinating tax liens;[13] doing so may have the effect of satisfying unsecured claimants, so that any deficiency claim does not necessarily diminish their recovery, or satisfying the senior claims secured by the property and thereby reducing or eliminating the deficiency.

Having identified and collected the property of the estate and established the claims and priorities in that property, it is the trustee's duty to oversee the orderly sale and liquidation of the estate, which also may entail surrender of the property to a secured creditor. Surrender of such property is required *prior* to the final distribution,[14] so that senior liens are satisfied before distribution to general unsecured claimants begins.

The actual mechanics of liquidation can be complicated. Liquidation sales raise the same concerns regarding both procedure and adequate and proper valuation discussed earlier in this text. Normally, actions of the trustee, unlike those of some debtors, are not of great concern, given the trustee's position as both a neutral and quasi-expert officer of the court. One might still challenge the sufficiency of the procedures, of course, but self-interest would not be at issue, or assumed, and therefore some obvious mistake (for example, insufficient notice of the sale or the use of a faulty collateral description) would have to occur for a procedural challenge to have a good likelihood of success.

Valuation is a potentially different matter. As we have seen, valuation is the critical element in the disposition of property, and potentially even more so in the case of a total liquidation. At the same time, it is uniquely subject to contrary and competing opinions, even given the likely and commonly anticipated receipt of lower prices than an ordinary course transaction at market value would realize. Higher priority claimants can expect this to be a source of challenge, particularly in cases in which the expected asset value of the debtor is substantially less than the aggregate value of the claims against it. Likewise, lower priority claimants in such cases will want to question valuations where possible and practical, given the direct relationship between higher valuations and higher payouts.

Distribution of the property remaining after surrender is subject to the following order of payment:[15]

- Administrative and priority claims, and unsecured claims, under the standard order of priorities established by Section 507 (see Section 3.2.5 above);
- Unsecured claims not covered by Section 507, with special treatment of tardily filed claims;
- Claims for fines, penalties, and punitive damages, to the extent they do not represent a claim for actual damages, which would be included among the higher priority claims above (and recall that these are the claims whose associated liens may be avoided by the trustee);
- Post-petition interest "at the legal rate;" and, finally,
- Any residual monies or property are returned to the debtor.

There are two issues to observe about the claim for post-petition interest allowed here. First, recall from our earlier discussions that in normal circumstances, and in particular in reorganizations under Chapter 11, post-petition interest is payable on fully secured claims only. The provision for payment of post-petition interest in a liquidation case therefore represents an *additional* allowance not otherwise available.[16] But note that the priority accorded to interest ranks only above residual recovery due the debtor after the satisfaction of all preceding claims; in other words, as a practical matter, recovery of post-petition interest in a liquidation is relatively uncommon.

Second, where payment for post-petition interest can be expected, the "legal rate" reference is again undefined, raising the same issues of determination we encountered previously in our discussion of post-petition interest calculations. As before, one would normally resort to the contract rate, if applicable, or an appropriate market index.[17]

One question that might have arisen by now concerns the handling of multiple claims of a given class. Particularly in larger, more complex cases, it is common to see more than one claimant in each priority category. The nature of priorities, though, is to distinguish *between* claimant classes, not *within* them. The Code provides for pro rata distribution of multiple claims within a given priority category.[18] Thus, if the estate has $100,000 available for payment to a particular priority category, and Creditor 1 is owed $500,000 while Creditor 2 is owed $250,000, Creditor 1 receives $66,667 and Creditor 2 receives $33,333.

The final procedural consideration of bankruptcy concerns the availability of discharge, and on this topic there is a notable distinction between liquidation under Chapter 7 and reorganization under Chapter 11. The concept of the discharge, which operates to forgive all debts that are not satisfied in bankruptcy, has a lengthy historical provenance, as alluded to in Chapter 1 of this text. As a matter of public policy, discharge represents and embodies the "fresh start" that bankruptcy is intended to provide. In Chapter 7 cases, the Code states that the court "shall grant the debtor a discharge, unless the debtor is not an individual."[19] Yes, you are reading that correctly: A corporate debtor is not discharged following liquidation.

The implication of the denial of discharge (which, by the way, may be accomplished in an individual case where some form of systemic abuse, neglect, or dishonesty is involved) is to leave open to claimants applicable state law remedies for debt collection. Now, it is true that a liquidated corporate debtor is likely to have little in the way of an asset base following liquidation that creditors actually would be able to pursue. But from time to time a particular debtor may emerge with attachable assets, or circumstances of the case or the debtor's dealings permit so-called actions to "pierce the corporate veil," in other words to pursue the individual owners behind the corporation. Moreover, guarantors of the debtor corporation's debt would not be released and therefore would be subject to collection. Where vulnerabilities of this kind exist, the lack of a discharge upon liquidation creates a strong incentive to pursue reorganization under Chapter 11. It is thus important for both debtors and creditors to be aware of this distinction between the two procedures, and to assess its significance in the particular case at hand. But, as noted above, it is also a reason to liquidate before asset value is depleted by avoidable delay; if claims are satisfied in whole or in part before this occurs, there will be less in the way of undischarged debts with which to be concerned.

4.2 Reorganization Under Chapter 11

We turn now to consideration of the more widely recognized bankruptcy proceeding, the reorganization of the business under Chapter 11. Before looking at the mechanics of the reorganization, let us take a moment to review the policy bases of Chapter 11. First and foremost, the Code adopts a presumption in favor of the debtor's rehabilitation. This means that, unlike early historical experience, which often tended toward the punitive side of the continuum, the Code expressly favors forgiveness and a fresh start. Only cases involving some dishonesty or abuse will result in some form of punitive sanction. This position was adopted in the Chapter 13 proceeding, the individual debtor analog of Chapter 11, but recognition of the additional functions performed by corporate debtors reinforced the idea that Chapter 11 should favor rehabilitation. Specifically, corporations are both competitors and employers, both of which functions serve important economic and social purposes. Retaining a company as a viable competitor within its industry and economic landscape serves to minimize the concentration of market power in the hands of oligopolies or monopolies. And maintaining a stable employment base has obvious social and economic benefits.

Second, it is also important to recognize that reorganization under Chapter 11 facilitates a redistribution of interests. In part, this is intended to permit the widest possible participation in a settlement, and on terms that share gains and losses. In a strict liquidation setting, as we saw above, the order of priorities is fixed and the rule of absolute priority normally is observed. This means that each group of claimants in the priority hierarchy is satisfied in full before the next succeeding group receives even partial satisfaction. As we observed briefly in Chapter 2 above, this is not always the case in a reorganization, which requires broad participation among the claimants and therefore may result in the redistribution of recoveries from higher priority claimants in favor of lower priority claimants.

Third, as the foregoing implies, Chapter 11 is a *negotiation*. Priorities and the rights and powers that follow from them do exist. Some claimants, therefore, are more equal than others. But it is important for all to understand that these are only framework considerations and are not determinative of the outcome of the case. Given the public policy interests involved, there should be no confusion on anyone's part that the Code creates a process that will not resemble a "black box" mechanical approach to settlement, and indeed that a collective, consensus-driven approach is engineered into the system.

As noted previously, the Code provisions we covered in Chapters 2 and 3 are applicable to both liquidations, except as discussed in the preceding section, and reorganizations. Therefore, in this section we will be considering the issues that are central to reorganizations alone, specifically those dealing with the development and confirmation of the plan of reorganization. We will from time to time refer back to those earlier provisions in order to provide context specific to their role in reorganizations, but other than introducing a few new procedural matters we will be concerned primarily with how a reorganization case is finalized.

4.2.1 Commencement of the Case

Commencement of the reorganization begins with the petition, or upon conversion from a Chapter 7 proceeding. But as we noted above in Section 4.1, the distinction between liquidations and reorganizations begins at the point of inception with the handling of the debtor's business and the status of the trustee. Whereas a trustee is appointed upon the commencement of a Chapter 7 case, in Chapter 11 the debtor becomes the debtor-in-possession and assumes the rights, powers, and duties of a trustee. This means that the debtor organization initially retains incumbent management to continue to operate the business *and* administer the estate in the bankruptcy proceeding. The policy behind this treatment again is based upon the rehabilitative purpose of the Code, and the assumption that existing management is in the best position to run the business. Lest this seem like too much of a potential conflict of interest in the bankruptcy case, note that the debtor-in-possession (again, the DIP, as it is referred to in bankruptcy practice) is obligated to perform the standard duties of the trustee.[20] And in general, we should note that the DIP is not given carte blanche over the bankruptcy proceedings. The Code specifies the grounds on which the court may appoint a trustee for cause, including dishonesty or incompetence.[21] The court also may appoint a trustee if it simply believes it is in the best interests of the estate and the claimants to do so. If a trustee is appointed, any party with an interest in the case may petition within 30 days to conduct a vote in accordance with the voting procedures applicable to liquidations, as outlined above.

Despite this check on abuse, there should be no doubt that the right to continue in control of the debtor's business is an important, and powerful, tool in the hands of the debtor. As we will see, the DIP is given the first opportunity to propose the plan of reorganization, which can have the effect of shaping the rest of the negotiations and the entire settlement process. The authority of the DIP with respect to its business is also furthered by the entry of so-called First Day Orders that are issued by the court for a limited period of time in order to authorize the operations of the business, including such acts as meeting payroll and using cash collateral.[22] These First Day Orders are intended to ensure that the business can continue without interruption, but, like the right of plan proposal, can fundamentally shape the debtor's ongoing conduct and, more consequentially, the disposition of the case. All parties to a bankruptcy thus should be alert to the implications of these initial orders.

The other organizing function that occurs upon commencement of a Chapter 11 case is the appointment of creditors' committees. The U.S. Trustee is empowered to appoint a committee representing the unsecured creditors, as well as any other committees representing other claimants or the equity holders.[23] The court also may respond to a request by any party to appoint yet other committees in a particular case if it deems it necessary to do so. We have alluded to the existence and function of creditors' committees elsewhere, but remember that it is the function of these committees to negotiate on behalf of the claimant class they represent and to serve as an information conduit for the other members of the class. More critically, the committees have the power to seek investigation of the debtor or to petition the court for conversion to Chapter 7. Committees also may employ accountants, lawyers, and others to represent the interests of the committee in the proceedings. Taken together, these rights tend to counterbalance the DIP's powers, although as reorganizations become larger and more complex the increase in a committee's power may be diminished by the increasing likelihood of internal conflict and/ or the existence of other, potentially competing, committees. In theory, though, the committees represent the Code's answer to this problem of numbers by concentrating authority in and giving a prominent role to the committees.

4.2.2 *Executory Contracts*

4.2.2.1 General Rules

One critical component of the operation of the business during reorganization concerns the handling of what are known as executory, or unexpired and yet to be completed, contracts. Technically, the term is defined to mean a contract under which both parties "are so far unperformed that the failure of either to perform would be a material breach."[24] This means that both parties owe material obligations to one another; contracts under which one party has already performed, either substantially or fully, are not executory under this definition. Thus, if I hire a contractor to build an addition to my house, and pay up front, the contract is not executory, given that my obligation to pay has been fulfilled. If, on the other hand, I agree to pay 25% now and the balance upon completion, the contract would be executory.

Here is the significance of the distinction: In essence, the Code gives the DIP (or trustee) the right, subject to court approval, to assume or reject any executory contract or unexpired lease at any time prior to confirmation of the plan of reorganization.[25] Courts are unlikely to question the decision to assume or reject if there is a good faith basis that would be covered by application of the business judgment rule. Some courts are more lenient in the case of assumption than rejection, in effect imposing a higher standard on the latter (typically involving a test based on whether performance would be burdensome to the estate).[26] If the contract is in default, the debtor may not assume it unless the default is cured or adequate assurance of performance is given by the debtor.[27] An important caveat to note in connection with defaulted contracts is that a contract under which the bankruptcy filing itself is a default event will not be considered to be in default for purposes of the requirement of curing existing defaults. Only defaults pertaining to actual performance must be cured prior to assumption in bankruptcy.

The debtor may reject the contract as an initial matter in the proceedings, or after first assuming it. If the contract is not assumed, the rejection gives rise to a claim for pre-petition breach of contract; in other words, the contract is treated as though the bankruptcy filing had not intervened and the debtor's breach caused damages to the counterparty's expectations under the contract. The claim for breach then becomes a general unsecured claim in the bankruptcy proceeding.[28] On the other hand, if the contract is assumed and later rejected, the rejection gives rise to a claim for breach of contract that dates from the time of the rejection, and is treated as an administrative expense entitled to priority.[29] Returning again to my contractor, if the contract is executory and the contractor rejects it upon filing, I have a claim for breach of contract that is treated as a general unsecured claim as of the date "immediately before the date of the filing of the petition."[30] Note that this effectively limits my damage claim, because market conditions may have changed substantially between that date and the date of rejection. If, on the other hand, the contractor assumes our agreement in bankruptcy, but later rejects it, my claim dates from the time of rejection, and whether I'm better or worse off monetarily as a result probably depends upon how much more the contractor accomplishes, and how much more I pay, before the rejection. But at least now I have a priority claim.

These represent the basic rules of procedure relating to the rejection or assumption of executory contracts. Let's step back a moment and look at the forest instead of the trees. Recall again that the Code's underlying bias is the rehabilitation of the debtor. One way this can be accomplished is by permitting the debtor to terminate bad deals made prior to the bankruptcy. And, as we have just seen, this right does not just exist upon filing: The debtor can wait and see how markets change or circumstances develop, and only then make the decision to assume or reject, and even reject after assuming the contract. Thus, in cases involving contracts that are sensitive to market conditions, perhaps involving purchase or supply transactions that establish a fixed price over the life of the contract, one would expect to see the debtor retain its interest in contracts providing for favorable terms of exchange, even if these emerge only during the course of the bankruptcy proceedings. There is also the possibility that the debtor could use the implicit threat of rejection to obtain a better deal from the original counterparty or from others who might step in and act as substitutes. And in such cases, a decision made on the basis of market conditions likely would survive a challenge under the business judgment rule.

The potential downside to this rule, at least from a policy perspective, is that the counterparties obviously are less well off as a result of having their contractual expectations reduced to a general unsecured claim in the bankruptcy. On the other hand, an argument still can be made that it is economically inefficient, or at a minimum somewhat unjust, to allow a party to a contract to reap rewards that are more beneficial than would be available in the market, especially in a bankruptcy context when such economic surplus in effect comes out of the recovery of the other claimants. The debtor's bad judgment, or simple bad luck, thus would benefit a contractual claimant to the detriment of all others, causing a redistribution in favor of the contracting party. This necessarily would be the outcome of a rule taking the opposite position to the right of rejection, instead requiring that the debtor abide by any and all existing contractual obligations. One might counter that outcomes of this sort are no less redistributive than some other provisions of the Code, and that in many cases bad judgment and bad luck are precisely why a debtor files for bankruptcy protection in the first place; other claimants did not have to deal with a judgment-challenged or star-crossed debtor, and, if they chose to do so, could have offset their risk by imposing stricter terms on the debtor in the form of higher prices, costs, fees, etc. Indeed, this may be exactly why the contract looked the way it did, and now the Code allows the debtor to avoid the terms of the bargain struck outside of bankruptcy. These are valid observations, but the Code seems to take cognizance of arguments to the contrary based on the now-familiar policy preference favoring debtor rehabilitation.

4.2.2.2 Labor and Pension Agreements

In addition to these basic rules, there are two other contractual obligations of the debtor that are singled out for special treatment only in Chapter 11 cases. These concern collective bargaining agreements and obligations to the debtor's retirees, which are set forth in a contract and thus subject to rejection *if necessary*. But note the change in approach this statement implies: Standard contractual agreements generally may be rejected of right by the debtor, but labor and retiree agreements are not subject to control and automatic rejection by the debtor.

Many years ago, it was not uncommon for companies to enter Chapter 11 almost solely for the purpose of rejecting their collective bargaining agreements; Continental Airlines was held up as a notorious example of this practice, and as a result Congress tightened the contract rejection rules as they apply to the debtor's dealings with its unions. Under the Code now,[31] prior to petitioning the court to reject the collective bargaining agreement, the debtor must submit a proposal to the union covering the suggested modifications of the terms of the agreement, provide the union with all information "necessary to evaluate the proposal," and meet and negotiate in good faith to obtain a mutually satisfactory modification of the agreement.[32] And significantly, the business judgment rule will not suffice to justify rejection. Instead, the court may grant the debtor's petition to reject the collective bargaining agreement if: (1) the debtor made a proposal that fairly and equitably accommodated the union, other claimants, and the estate; (2) the union refused to accept the proposal without good cause; and (3) the "balance of the equities" clearly favors rejection.[33] The latter phrase can be thought of as shorthand for whatever the court deems to be the most sympathetic argument, taking basic fairness into consideration. The recent GM and Chrysler bankruptcies essentially involved the use of these provisions to provide compensation to the unions, in the form of additional equity participation in the reorganized companies, in exchange for modification of the companies' pre-petition labor agreements. Out and out rejection, then, is unlikely to be permitted in any but the most extreme circumstances, perhaps where the company cannot survive without more than a modification of the existing terms. The GM and Chrysler cases, which arguably served to illustrate the fate of companies in dire straits (due at least in part to their collective bargaining agreements), may establish precedents for the treatment of similar cases in the future.

The other kind of contract now subject to special treatment in reorganizations is the retiree benefit agreement. Retirees are entitled to representation in the bankruptcy, either by "a labor organization" or by such other party as the court, following a motion by any interested party, may determine is appropriate.[34] If the debtor is proposing to modify or suspend payment to the retirement plan, the court must appoint a committee to represent the interests of any retirees not covered by a collective bargaining agreement. The debtor is required to continue making contributions to the retirement plan, without modification, unless authorized by the court, and must make the same kind of proposal for modification and provide the same information required of the debtor with respect to collective bargaining agreements. The court may then authorize the modification, again on the same bases required above in connection with labor negotiations. The court also may order an interim modification, in other words prior to the conclusion of a permanent modification as just discussed, if it would be essential to the debtor's business or in order to avoid irreparable damage to the estate.[35]

To summarize briefly, debtors may assume or reject executory contracts. Special rules regarding timing and procedure may apply to certain kinds of contracts, but generally speaking the debtor must cure existing defaults before assuming the contract. And if the debtor rejects the contract, the counterparty's claim is entered in the bankruptcy as a general unsecured claim for breach of contract. The permissive right to reject does not apply to collective bargaining or retirement benefit agreements, which, as we saw, require the input of the affected workers or retirees in order to modify.

We turn now to consideration of the most important part of the reorganization process, the development, negotiation, and confirmation of the plan. Once again, keep in mind as we work through this material that the plan represents a negotiation between the debtor and its claimants. Rights and powers are given to both sides by the Code in order to balance their respective interests, but there is no determinative force associated with one's status beyond those basic rights and powers. The circumstances of the case may favor one or more of the parties involved and accordingly confer more influence over the proceedings based on their status, but the outcome is still subject to negotiation and approval as a collective endeavor among the parties involved.

4.2.3 Development and Acceptance of the Plan

The basic pattern of plan development and confirmation is simple enough: A plan is proposed that addresses all claimant classes by providing for a settlement of their claims, the creditors vote to approve or reject, and if approved the plan is confirmed by the court and the case is closed. As usual, though, general descriptions of the process mask the complexity involved. We will consider a few of the complexities surrounding the plan in the discussion to follow by looking at the major components of the process from start to finish.

4.2.3.1 Classification of Claims

For a plan to be meaningful, there must be some distinction made between and among different kinds of claims. Think about the dealings and interactions of any large, and many moderate-sized, businesses and you can get a sense of what this means. There will be a multiplicity of different kinds and amounts of claims with which the debtor must deal. Broadly speaking, we can return to our priority list (see Chapter 3) for guidance as to the composition of each general category, but even these may be insufficient to describe all of the interests involved. In this case, we would further subdivide the general category into one or more classes of that kind.

In accomplishing this division of interests, the Code itself provides minimal guidance, stating simply that "a plan may place a claim or interest in a particular class only if such claim or interest is substantially similar" to the other claims in that class.[36] No definition of "substantially similar" is given. Naturally, it is impossible to provide an explicit definition of terms of this kind that will always clarify the relevant factors of every case, and the Code drafters, as in many other instances, sought to promulgate a broad principle rather than a specific rule. But as we also have seen in other such instances of relative vagueness, there is some room for strategic application, and sometimes not in ways that necessarily were intended. Given the voting rules we will discuss later and the fact that the debtor is given first right to propose a plan, the classification of interests is a matter of the debtor's definition that can open the door to selective classification.

Consider the following scenario in evaluating potential claim classifications. Suppose that Supermann, Inc., files under Chapter 11. Among its many creditors is Luthor Industries, with which Supermann has what might politely be called a toxic relationship. Luthor almost certainly will oppose anything that Supermann advocates. The nature of Luthor's claim is such that it might reasonably be placed in either of two classes, but if placed in one that contains another uncooperative claimant Luthor could tilt the balance of power against Supermann. Therefore, Supermann places the Luthor claim in the other class, which contains a number of friendly claimants, thereby isolating Luthor in the vote on the plan.

There is some controversy as to whether the possibility of claim gerrymandering is a weakness of the Code in practical application. First, it may be unlikely that a given claimant would be both similar to others in its class and also uniquely of a different perspective on the proposed settlement. Second, some also believe that in bankruptcies of any significant size, the complexity of the case swamps the ability to selectively classify claims. In many instances, this is undoubtedly true, but it is also possible that the increasing complexity of larger cases gives rise to more bases on which claim distinctions can be made. The point is that it remains possible under the Code to define claimant classifications opportunistically.

Notwithstanding these observations, it is important to stress here that the debtor cannot construct classes on a clearly arbitrary basis.[37] The "substantially similar" test, for example, would preclude grouping secured with unsecured claims (as would basic rules of prioritization, in this particular example), or more senior secured or unsecured claimants with junior secured or unsecured claimants. But secured creditors might be subject to classification on the basis of collateral, and certainly on time of perfection, and unsecured claims can contain many different kinds of obligations between the debtor and the claimants that can provide the basis for placing claims in different classes. And it should be emphasized that doing so is not always an attempt to manipulate the outcome of the reorganization; there may be valid business reasons for a particular classification approach that has more to do with maintenance of post-bankruptcy relationships than with a desire to harm a particular claimant. As is true of many issues under the Code, the facts of a specific case will determine whether or not the possibility of opportunism exists and whether its impact is likely to be significant. For our purposes, it is enough to highlight the possibility and remind readers to be aware of the issue in order to know when to use the provision or challenge its application.

4.2.3.2 Proposing the Plan; Exclusivity

The debtor is given the first opportunity to propose a plan, and may even file it with the petition. In most cases, this does not occur and the plan is negotiated in the proceedings. Most significantly, *only* the debtor may develop and propose a plan during the first 120 days of the case.[38] This is known as the exclusivity period, to which we have referred previously, and its import is to enable the debtor to substantially shape the terms of the Chapter 11 negotiation. The Code also provides for a 180-day window of exclusivity if the debtor proposes a plan within 120 days but has not secured approval. Thus, the debtor may file its plan on day 120 and secure an additional 60 days in which to seek approval. These windows may or may not be absolute, for any party may petition for an increase or decrease in the applicable window; debtors obviously would seek to extend the allowed time while claimants would seek shorter time periods. No guidelines are provided in the Code with respect to the court's discretion in lengthening or shortening the period of exclusivity, other than imposing an absolute limit of 18 months (20 if the petition is made within the 180-day window[39]), but this is the provision that enables some debtors to remain in control of plan development for an extensive period, often beyond the point that creditors might be willing to wait to receive a settlement.

Only if the debtor has not filed a plan within 120 days or secured approval within 180 days (assuming no extensions are granted, per above) may the claimants file alternative plans. This provides some leverage in the case to counterbalance the debtor's control during the exclusivity period. If claimants object to the plan offered by the debtor, they may withhold their consent in order to exhaust exclusivity, then file their own plans and seek approval. Whether it is in their interests to play a waiting game, particularly if there is a reasonable likelihood that the debtor can secure an extension, is an issue to be determined in each case, but this is the specification of the reorganization game: The debtor's exclusivity on the one hand, possibly augmented by extensions, balanced against the claimants' ability to withhold consent and wait for exclusivity to lapse, on the other. Both sides must calibrate their approaches to plan development with the others' positions in mind.

4.2.3.3 Contents of the Plan

The Code specifies plan contents, including both mandatory and permissive items.[40] In the case of mandatory elements, for our purposes the key

provisions are the designation of claims, as discussed above, the identification of impaired and unimpaired classes, the treatment of impaired
classes, and the selection of officers. We will discuss the latter point in
connection with governance issues in Chapter 5, but note simply that this
is where the interests of plan confirmation and governance converge. The
plan also must show adequate means of implementation.

When we speak of impairment, we mean essentially that, as the term
suggests, a claim has been altered in some way, most commonly by the
proposed payment of less than the full amount due. Any alteration of any
contractual right of *any* claimant in a class constitutes impairment of the
class, unless the debtor proposes to cure the impairment as part of the settlement.[41] In the latter situation, the class would not be considered impaired. If
a class is impaired, the plan must provide for the proposed treatment of the
class, which requires detailed specification of the value to be distributed to
the impaired class, the property involved, and the timing of payment or conferral of additional interests (as where an additional lien might be proposed).
The distinction between impaired and unimpaired classes is important
because only the impaired classes vote on the plan, as we will discuss below.

The Code's treatment of permissive components includes a catchall
for "any other appropriate provision" beyond the specifically identified
matters, some or all of which may not apply to every case and may not
cover all the specifics with which the case must deal.[42] The enumerated
components include the treatment of executory contracts; the settlement
or adjustment of any claim belonging to the debtor or the estate, or in
other words the non-debt contractual or property rights of the debtor; the
sale of any estate property; or the modification of the rights of any secured
or unsecured claimant, which would include any non-monetary alteration of interests, as where a plan might propose the subordination of an
existing lien or an alteration in the time of repayment. Note also that this
alteration clause would constitute impairment and require elaboration of
how the debtor proposes to treat the class in the plan of reorganization.

4.2.3.4 Solicitation and Disclosure

The Code requires adherence to specific procedures relating to the physical distribution of the plan to the claimants and the solicitation of the

vote.[43] The process is formalized to minimize opportunities to exert any undue influence or hide material facts from the claimants. The debtor must provide each claimant with a copy of the plan and a written disclosure statement, which is similar to the issuance of prospectuses in connection with securities offerings in that the disclosure must provide "adequate information" pertaining to all of the debtor's property, finances, operations, etc.[44] The court may approve a disclosure statement, though, without requiring a valuation or appraisal of the debtor's property, and different disclosure statements may be issued to the different classes (although the same statement must be provided to all claimants within a class). For these and other reasons, the reorganization disclosure may differ substantially from what would be required under otherwise applicable securities laws governing disclosure.[45]

4.2.3.5 Voting on the Plan

The final stage of the plan development process, and arguably the most important, involves the claimants' vote to accept or reject the proposed plan. Voting rights are specified in the Code, which we will elaborate shortly, but the general requirements for voting acceptance can be stated as follows:[46]

- Each holder of a claim must accept the plan or have been forced to do so under the Code's "cramdown" provision; and
- Each impaired class must accept the plan.

Before we begin our look at actual voting mechanics and requirements, note first that the vote represents a claimant's best opportunity to block plan confirmation, as long as that claimant can sway the class of which it is a part or represents the swing vote within the class. It is at this stage that everyone needs to understand a central dynamic: Although the structure of the Code, following standard procedures of corporate law liquidation priorities, creates an environment in which the rule of absolute priority can be maintained, in fact many reorganizations break absolute priority.[47] This can occur for a variety of reasons, from a debtor's desire to favor some groups of creditors over others to the claimants' own ability to withhold consent to a plan pending some concession from the debtor, other claimants, or both. Hence the importance of structuring the classes and crafting the proposed plan, because the initial proposal may, as we have suggested on several occasions, condition the parties' positions with respect to the plan and therefore the final outcome itself. In maximizing one's opportunities arising from this dynamic, it is important to consider the ability of some or all parties to hold out for a different proposal; the ability to defeat exclusivity and draft an alternative plan; the position one occupies within a class given the voting requirements elaborated below; and the availability of challenge points within the plan or the process as a whole, especially including our old friend, valuation. These and any other case-specific dynamics can lead to a materially different reorganization outcome.

The first issue in the voting process to consider is the treatment of unimpaired classes. As we mentioned above, unimpaired classes are conclusively deemed to accept the plan, and no vote takes place. Remember that a class is considered unimpaired if the plan leaves its contractual rights unaltered, or cures certain defaults. While this sounds fine in principle, the catch for a creditor is that the right to cure carries with it the abrogation of the creditor's right to accelerate the payment of the debt upon default.[48] In turn, this may mean some claims for collection (default interest, for example) are impaired, but the Code treats this as an instance of an unimpaired claim and the creditor is unable to vote against the plan as a result. Thus, the debtor may be able in some cases to use this provision to terminate some claimant rights and still obtain plan approval.

In the opposite case, where a claimant class is denied any recovery under the plan, the class is deemed to *reject* the plan. Issues of acceptance and confirmation will be discussed in the following section, as will the possibility that the debtor might, say, attempt to give nothing to a particular class of unsecured creditors so that equity holders might be able to recover something on their investments. For now, it is sufficient to be aware that not all claimant classes must receive a settlement (even apart from equity holders, who commonly receive little or nothing given their low priority status), and that no vote is required of them given the presumption of rejection.

It is in the "middle" set of claims, those that are impaired but still allocated some settlement under the plan, that the right to vote resides and where the battle is joined. As we discussed in our consideration of claim classification above, a class is composed of similar kinds of claims, and it is the class that votes as a whole and which must give its assent in any case (we will consider the qualification of the individual claimant's vote shortly). But it is not a simple majority that is sufficient to establish class acceptance. Rather, an affirmative vote must be secured from holders of at least two- thirds in amount and one-half in number of the total claims represented in the class.[49]

Consider the following hypothetical set of claims and classes:

- Class 1: Five claimants holding claims of $250,000, $200,000, $150,000, $100,000, and $50,000.
- Class 2: Two claimants holding claims of $100,000 each.
- Class 3: Four claimants, two holding claims of $200,000 each and two holding claims of $100,000 each.

For now we will assume that the division of these claims into classes is appropriate and that no gerrymandering has occurred. The votes required by class would be as follows:

- Class 1: Three claimants and $500,000 of claims;
- Class 2: Both claimants; and
- Class 3: Three claimants and $400,000 of claims.

Within each class, any permutation of the claimants resulting in the requisite number and value of claims will suffice, but in an actual case the identity of these parties may be critical to the achievement of acceptance. For example, if we return to our battle between Supermann, Inc., and Luthor Industries, if Luthor holds the largest claim in Class 1, *all* of the other claimants must vote to accept, whereas if Luthor holds the smallest claim, only Three of the others will be necessary if one of them is the largest claim. Likewise, Supermann's reorganization would be in deep trouble if Luthor were part of Class 2, given the equal status of the two claimants. Without joint acceptance of these claimants, the amount of claims requirement cannot be satisfied even though the number of claims requirement would be.

At this juncture, an interesting simulation might be developed following this outline or with some variation to allow participants to experience the dynamics of plan proposal and voting acceptance. Note again that these are the two critical steps in the process, because the composition of the class may be an important determinant of its vote. No specification of the contents of the plan proposal is given here since we are primarily concerned with voting dynamics, but these may be supplied in order to permit the alteration of specific settlement offers necessary to obtain consent.

Indeed, this latter point is critical to an appreciation of voting dynamics, because all parties involved must identify the critical claimants, those who hold the balance of power within a class either because of the size of their claim or of the class, or because of the breakdown of the other votes in the class. Holdouts exert their influence at this stage of the process through this balance of power mechanism. It is important, then, to understand not only who these claimants are but what their interests are in order to propose an alternative that would be more acceptable than the present plan. Equally important, of course, is an understanding of when such claimants actually cannot press their advantage, for example where they remain the sole holdout and are subject to cramdown, which we investigate in the following section.

Assuming the vote has been satisfactorily resolved, the plan is accepted and attention shifts to the final confirmation of the plan. This is a separate step from the vote to accept and involves different tests and requirements. Claimants who are not satisfied with the vote may be able to challenge confirmation. The difference is that voting involves an exercise in counting, while confirmation is a legal matter; any party challenging confirmation of the approved plan must be able to raise a specific objection relevant to any of the requirements for confirmation outlined in the Code. We will turn to these issues in the section to follow.

4.2.4 Confirmation of the Plan and Discharge

4.2.4.1 General Rules

As implied above, confirmation of the plan is not automatic upon its acceptance under the Code's voting procedures. The Code specifies a number of requirements that must be met in order for an accepted plan to be confirmed.[50] The most important of these requirements for our purposes are the following:

- Each class must either be unimpaired or have voted to accept the plan.
- Any claimant voting against the plan must, under the plan, receive the present value of its recovery under a Chapter 7 liquidation.
- At least one impaired class must have voted to accept the plan.
- Confirmation must not be likely to be followed by liquidation or additional reorganization.

The Code strives for a consensus in favor of the plan, and thus its voting mechanics and these confirmation tests can only be satisfied under such consensus. Remember that unimpaired classes are conclusively deemed to accept the plan, so the actual vote of the impaired classes in favor of the plan is the critical component of this test. Individual or class holdouts, implicit in the second and third requirements of this list, are subject to cramdown as discussed below, but the requirement that at least one impaired class approve the plan again allows for, and requires, general consensus (at least on the assumption that the non-consenting classes still are subject to cramdown).

The requirement of feasibility, represented by the fourth test above, is subjective. The debtor bears the burden of satisfying the court that no liquidation or additional reorganization will follow. In practice, companies not infrequently resort to Chapter 22 or even Chapter 33 reorganizations, in other words two or more successive reorganizations. The Code does not specify a projected time limit for consideration of feasibility, and the occurrence of repeat filings therefore suggests that a mere showing that the business *can* survive on the terms provided in the plan is sufficient to carry the question. No representation that a repeat filing will not occur within one, two, or five years is required.

4.2.4.2 Cramdown

Let's assume that the debtor is able to satisfy all requirements for confirmation other than the unanimity requirements of class or individual holders. In that case, the Code's cramdown provision is triggered.[51]

Cramdown, so-called because of the imagery of forcing something down an unwilling party's throat, permits confirmation of a plan notwithstanding a holdout by a class or an individual claimant if the plan does not discriminate unfairly against any dissenting class or claimant and also is fair and equitable in its treatment of their claims.

In turn, the test of a fair and equitable disposition of claims differs depending on whether we are dealing with secured or unsecured claims.[52] Secured claimants must be allowed by the plan to: (1) retain the underlying lien and receive deferred payments that satisfy the obligation; (2) retain a lien on the proceeds of any property sold free and clear of the underlying lien; or (3) otherwise receive the "indubitable equivalent" of the value of the claim. The first possible settlement option represents essentially a status quo arrangement of payment secured by the existing lien, while the second allows for the possibility of selling the property outright to raise cash but allowing the creditor's lien interest to attach first to the sales proceeds. The third alternative is a catchall provision, allowing other contingencies to develop in a specific case as long as the creditor's interest is maintained in some fashion. As we have seen elsewhere, the ultimate question to be settled is the precise nature of "indubitable equivalent" as applied to a specific proposal.

In the case of unsecured claims, a plan proposal is fair and equitable if: (1) the plan offers the claimant the amount of the claim in question, or (2) no junior interest receives any settlement. The first of these conditions addresses the problem of a holdout looking for a better settlement or an additional concession (e.g., nomination of a member of the board). Of course, not all reorganizations will allow for satisfaction in full of the claims against the estate. When this is the case, the junior interest exclusion gives the claimant protection against unfair treatment while allowing the debtor to gain confirmation by giving something to everyone who is entitled to a settlement. For example, suppose we have five claimant classes, the first three of which in order of priority are satisfied in full. The fourth and fifth classes involve unsecured claims. We do not like the members of our fourth class and therefore seek to dramatically underfund the settlement of their claims, while also giving more to members of the fifth class with which we hope to do business following the reorganization. Under the fair and equitable standard, this proposal fails since we have not paid the fourth class the value of its claims and a junior class receives a settlement. Note that this outcome mirrors the concept of absolute priority in requiring satisfaction of a higher priority set of claims. If, on the other hand, we alter our proposal, not by giving the fourth class the full value of its claims but simply by adding the amount we intended to pay the fifth class to the sum we offer to the fourth class, the plan will pass the fair and equitable test. Under this revision, the fifth class does not receive anything on its claims, which is sufficient to trigger cramdown and permit confirmation.

Having attained confirmation of the plan by one of these methods, either by vote or by cramdown, the debtor's case is closed and unsettled obligations are discharged in full.[53] Readers will recall that no discharge is available in a liquidation case, a major distinction between the two regimes. In Chapter 11, the discharge eliminates any non-plan obligations as if they had never arisen, leaving only the obligations remaining under the plan. In effect, the plan obligations are substituted for the presumably larger class of obligations owed by the debtor prior to bankruptcy. Note how this outcome achieves the policy goal of the Code: The debtor is given a modified set of obligations, all of which have been negotiated and are (theoretically) acceptable to all and manageable for the debtor. Prepetition obligations, at least some of which were (theoretically) unmanageable in light of the need for reorganization, are either rationalized as part of the bankruptcy settlement or expunged. Chapter 7, by contrast, does not contemplate the need for a fresh start, but instead looks to an orderly unwinding and dissolution of the debtor's affairs. Thus, disallowing discharge does not threaten the debtor's post-bankruptcy existence and permits the continuing settlement of pre-petition obligations to the extent possible.

This concludes our look at the bankruptcy processes of liquidation and reorganization. The following chapter discusses the application of the general bankruptcy framework to a number of specific issues and contexts.

CHAPTER 5

Special Topics

In this chapter, we will look at a number of different topics that may or may not be involved in the typical case and which are not part of the formal bankruptcy mechanics with which we were concerned previously. Nevertheless, these topic areas may be of some importance where they do arise, and indeed may even raise the central issue or issues of the case, and therefore are deserving of attention. That said, it should be noted that the purpose of this chapter is not to provide comprehensive coverage of these topics, but rather to offer a survey of their implications for, and treatment in, bankruptcy proceedings. We will consider in turn the recent Code revisions applicable to small business bankruptcies; prepackaged bankruptcies; the implications of organizational structure and form; the purchase and sale of claims; governance issues in bankruptcy; and the treatment of derivatives.

5.1 Small Business Bankruptcies

Recall from Chapter 1 that the Bankruptcy Act of 1898 included separate provisions for large, public corporations (Chapter X) and private firms, which usually were small businesses (Chapter XI). With the Code's enactment in 1978, these provisions were folded into a single set of rules applicable to any debtor meeting the fundamental eligibility criteria, regardless of size. This unitary structure was changed by the BAPCPA (2005).

BAPCPA's primary focus, and the object of most popular press accounts, was a tightening of the treatment of and procedures applicable to individual bankruptcies, which made it harder to achieve a full discharge and required credit counseling, among the more notable changes. As its full name suggests, BAPCPA was enacted on the assumption that bankruptcy was being abused by many individual debtors who irresponsibly and unconscionably incurred unmanageable debt burdens, only to use bankruptcy to evade the necessity of repayment. Whether the underlying assumption was true or not, and certainly there were at least some debtors who fit the profile, the result was a marked shift toward creditor control of individual bankruptcy cases.

Less noted was BAPCPA's *de facto* reversion to the Bankruptcy Act's approach to large and small business bankruptcies, ostensibly for the same anti-fraud purposes underlying the act's individual debtor amendments. The logic behind these amendments seems to be the following: Small businesses commonly are owned and run by individuals, and individuals are more likely than large businesses to abuse the system, ergo small businesses need additional oversight in bankruptcy. Broadly speaking, BAPCPA restores the distinction between large and small businesses found in the old Bankruptcy Act, and arguably imposes a more rigid set of compliance and reporting requirements on small businesses than on large corporations. The effect of these changes on small business behavior, both in general and in the shadow of bankruptcy remains to be seen; without a streamlined system available, small business debtors may approach financial distress differently than they would have in the past. In turn, this may lead to inefficiencies or misallocation of resources in the entrepreneurial sector of the economy that did not exist before. Only time will tell.

For all intents and purposes, the small business provisions are operational only in Chapter 11 cases. They do apply to Chapter 7 proceedings, but the different context there negates a number of specific requirements that must be observed in reorganization. Under the BAPCPA amendments, a "small business debtor" is one whose secured and unsecured obligations do not exceed $2,190,000.[1] Note that the threshold is phrased in terms of debt rather than assets. Given a presumption of insolvency, the small business debtor's assets normally would be expected to be equal to or less than the amount given in the definition, but this is not necessarily always true. And of greater import is the structural incentive the definition provides: Assets may or may not be subject to short-term adjustment, but debts might be incurred with the sole purpose of avoiding classification as a small business debtor. It is the debtor's obligation to note its status as a small business debtor, a designation that can be challenged by any other party in the case.[2]

Upon filing the petition, the small business debtor must also include its most recent financial information and meet with the U.S. Trustee.[3] It is the U.S. Trustee's job to screen the debtor and determine whether the debtor reasonably can be expected to complete reorganization, and to move for dismissal where the U.S. Trustee determines that a reorganization cannot be successfully concluded. Assuming dismissal is not ordered by the court, the small business debtor is required to make periodic financial disclosures throughout the pendency of the case, allow the U.S. Trustee to inspect its properties and records and otherwise make itself subject to oversight by the U.S. Trustee, and maintain insurance "customary and appropriate to the industry." These requirements are not specifically imposed on large businesses by the Code. The small business debtor, however, is allowed to use a simplified form of disclosure for purposes of soliciting the vote on a proposed plan of reorganization.

In terms of management of the case itself, probably the most significant alteration in the standard bankruptcy procedure applicable to the small business debtor concerns the exclusivity period. Recall that this is the period of time following the filing of the petition within which the debtor is allowed the exclusive right to formulate and propose a plan of reorganization. In a small business case, the period of exclusivity is shortened to 180 days, and the plan and disclosure statement must be filed within 300 days. Extensions may be granted by the court only if the debtor establishes that it is more likely than not that a confirmable plan will be proposed, a new deadline is imposed at the time the extension is granted, and the extension occurs prior to the expiration of the statutory period.[4] The latter condition precludes the possibility of waiting until the last few weeks to seek extension in order to take advantage of the normal backlog of cases experienced in most jurisdictions, which further shortens the effective exclusivity or plan development window. These timeframes should be compared to the 18–20 month window possible in cases that do not involve designated small businesses. To some extent, there is a justification for shortening the applicable window in order to facilitate conclusion of what should be relatively simpler cases; longer periods of time are more likely to be necessary in large and complex reorganizations, and in either case are more expensive to administer. But the overall effect of the amendments to exclusivity is to deny the small business debtor the opportunity to control its destiny to the same extent a large corporation may under the Code.

There is one contingency that applies to designation as a small business debtor that allows a debtor otherwise falling within the statutory definition to avoid its coverage: If a creditors' committee is formed that the court believes will be effective, the case will not be handled under the small business provisions.[5] In effect, the U.S. Trustee's heightened oversight is intended to substitute for that of a committee, which in most very small bankruptcy cases will not be formed or active as a consequence of normal cost-benefit calculations (a small case not being worth the time and effort of meeting, strategizing, etc.). Note that this provides an incentive for the debtor to engage in some form of negotiated arrangement with one or more creditors to sit as a committee in the case. While this allows an outlet for the small business concerned by the potential effects of the BAPCPA amendments, it is undoubtedly going to come at the cost of giving greater leverage to the creditors, a cost that larger businesses do not need to bear.

Again, only time will tell what the impact of the small business amendments will be. One can envision pre-petition decisions that will be made solely because of a desire to avoid designation as a small business. The changes enacted by BAPCPA also would seem designed to alter at least some post-petition dynamics, often by limiting the debtor's discretion and giving more power to the claimants. It is unclear as an empirical matter why small businesses alone should be singled out for such treatment.

5.2 Pre-packaged Bankruptcies

Pre-packaged bankruptcies, or pre-packs, are those in which the negotiations otherwise conducted in the normal Chapter 11 proceeding occur in the pre-petition environment. Upon concluding the negotiations and reaching agreement on a plan, the debtor then is in position to file its bankruptcy petition and obtain virtually simultaneous confirmation. Thus, compared to a standard reorganization proceeding, a pre-pack normally is faster, at least as to time actually spent in court and under court supervision. The Code explicitly contemplates pre-packs by allowing the plan to be filed with the petition[6] and by giving binding effect to pre-petition solicitation and votes.[7] The only condition is that the solicitation process must be consistent with any applicable non-bankruptcy laws governing the process (such as securities laws relating to disclosure).

If everything is worked out ahead of time, one might ask, why bother with the bankruptcy petition at all? It certainly is possible to negotiate the equivalent of a reorganization plan with the organization's claimants, but in many instances this may be accomplished, if at all, only in piecemeal fashion. Moreover, if one or more claimants are not amenable to a proposed settlement, nothing outside of bankruptcy compels them to negotiate, much less accept its terms. Recall that in Chapter 11, confirmation of a plan is possible even over the objection of dissenting claimants. A pre-pack offers the opportunity to negotiate with willing parties, and then use the power of the bankruptcy court to enforce the provisions of the agreed plan on holdouts via the cramdown process. Finally, the availability of discharge makes the conclusion of the case in bankruptcy more appealing than in a non-judicial setting in which holdouts can still pursue their claims.

Consequently, pre-packs usually are a good tool in cases in which more claimants than not are willing to negotiate and when the number of claimant interests is relatively limited. Note that this is not necessarily a question of the absolute number of creditors, but rather the ease with which their interests can be aggregated within class groupings in order to facilitate the negotiating process and simplify the proposed settlement. Where the debtor's affairs give rise to a multiplicity of claims and interests, there may be little advantage to negotiating a pre-pack instead of filing a bankruptcy petition and organizing the multiple layers of claims and interests in a traditional Chapter 11 framework. The advantages offered by a pre-pack also may be limited where certain claimants already are pursuing, or threatening to pursue, remedies against the debtor; in such circumstances, it may be advantageous to file and gain the protection of the automatic stay (which arguably was the problem encountered by the Texas Rangers, as we saw in Chapter 1). The facts of the specific case alone can determine whether a pre-pack or a traditional bankruptcy proceeding is preferable.

5.3 Organizational Structure: Subsidiaries and Franchises

From time to time in our elaboration of the Code we referred to the implications associated with the structural form of the debtor. In particular, we noted the potential advantages that might accrue to a company organized as parent to a variety of subsidiaries in deciding where to file. We also took note of cases in which some, but not all, of the entities within a corporate family seek bankruptcy protection. In this section we will consider some of the problems associated with complex organizations, typically involving multiple subsidiaries, that engage in intra-corporate transactions or transactions with third parties. Buyout transactions, such as leveraged buyouts or private equity transactions, previously discussed in conjunction with the doctrine of equitable subordination, raise additional concerns that are related to structure and internal dealings, and also will be discussed here. Finally, we will talk briefly about another commonly encountered structural form, franchising, and some of the special issues it raises in bankruptcy.

Consider first a company with three subsidiaries. One is doing fairly well, but the other two are in varying stages of distress, and consequently so is the parent when viewed as a consolidated entity. Legally, though, we are dealing with four separate enterprises, each of which may transact business and incur debt independently of the others. In this scenario, let us assume that the healthy subsidiary is held out of the proceedings, while the parent and its other subsidiaries file under Chapter 11. What are the potential ramifications of this kind of arrangement?

First, dealings between and among the components of the corporate group should be analyzed. Suppose that the corporate parent in this scenario had rearranged the corporate assets in order to make sure the most valuable properties were held by the strong subsidiary. Even if this was done without intent to defraud, any such transactions may be attacked as fraudulent transfers if they meet the specific conditions that we outlined in Chapter 3. Suppose, though, that our parent debtor is devious and smart. Realizing that the Code imposes a two-year limitation period on transfers involving actual fraud, the parent undertakes the transactions, waits for the two-year window to lapse, and then files a bankruptcy petition. What result? Now, claimants actually would not be able to avail themselves of the Code's fraudulent transfer provisions. But all is not lost: As an additional remedy, one that was not essential to the presentation of basic fraudulent transfer mechanics in Chapter 3 and therefore deferred until now, claimants may be able to use the Code's fraudulent transfer provisions to apply state law and extend the limitation period to as much as four years.[8] Again, a devious debtor, knowing even this, might still defer filing, but practically speaking the longer the window the less manipulation is likely to take place.

Second, depending upon the facts of the case and the nature of any transactions among the members of the corporate group, it may be possible to challenge the selective bankruptcies of the parent and the weak subsidiaries. The goal here would be to pull the healthy subsidiary into the proceedings, not just assets that might have been fraudulently transferred. Achieving this outcome may require a showing that the dealings among the parties were such that the corporate form dividing their interests is a sham, and that all of the entities can and should be considered a single debtor for purposes of the bankruptcy. Even if a legitimate interest and business purpose is served in separating the entities, and all formalities are observed, it still may be possible to argue for the inclusion of all entities on an "enterprise" theory, according to which there is no practical economic separation of interests and all entities enjoy and confer common benefits. In the alternative, one might use similar facts to seek dismissal of the case; this would frustrate the debtor's likely intent and permit claimants to pursue non-bankruptcy remedies, possibly against the healthy subsidiary as well. At the very least, such an approach may be sufficient to exert leverage against the debtor and obtain necessary concessions. Finally, if the conditions are met, claimants should not overlook the possibility of forcing an involuntary case upon any excluded corporate entities.

If we look at the structure of many complex entities, we often find not only dealings between and among the component entities but also between the group as a whole and third parties. Often seeking to avoid problems such as those just discussed, creditors may seek to attach the assets of all corporate entities precisely so that a shell game cannot ensue. From time to time, though, this practice raises problems of its own. For example, it is not uncommon to secure cross-guarantees and/or cross-collateralized obligations of the various corporate entities. In this arrangement, indebtedness incurred by one entity gives creditors recourse across the corporate family. This may be a practical response to the prospect of losing assets somewhere among the various entities, but it creates a fraudulent or preferential transfer issue: At least as to guarantees or collateralization of the parent's or a corporate sibling's obligations by another subsidiary, there is a risk that a court may find that the granting of that interest was not given in exchange for value. In other words, the subsidiary gave something away but may not have received anything in return, or only indirectly as a member of the corporate group. Interests granted by the parent on behalf of its subsidiaries, though, usually can survive challenge on these grounds on the presumption that benefits flowing to the subsidiaries as part of the financing arrangement also flow upward to the parent.

Fraudulent transfer theory also has been applied to leveraged buyout transactions. We have previously discussed the possibility that these deals may give rise to a claim for equitable subordination. In a leveraged buyout, of course, the corporation purchased by new ownership pledges its assets as security for indebtedness used to fund the transaction. The debtor corporation often is rendered technically insolvent as a result, and therefore constructive fraud can be claimed under the Code's treatment of fraudulent transfers.[9] If so, the transaction (specifically, the grant of collateral) can be avoided and other claimants can attach the assets of the debtor. It should be noted again that many private equity transactions today may be subject to a similar analysis. Such transactions commonly make use of so-called "dividend recapitalizations," in which substantial sums are borrowed against the portfolio company's assets and then distributed to the private equity owners—often prior to an initial public offering.[10] If the portfolio firms are rendered insolvent as a result of the recapitalization, the Code's fraudulent transfer provisions could be triggered.

The last "structural" form to be considered involves franchising, a popular business model in today's economy. The franchisee and franchisor are separate entities, both legally and practically, in a way that a corporate parent and its subsidiaries are not. But clearly there is a joint purpose and a relationship between the two that is founded in contract in the form of the franchise agreement. Moreover, the base franchise agreement may have been supplemented by a variety of other contracts, such as development or procurement contracts.[11] As far as the Code is concerned, then, a bankruptcy by either franchisee or franchisor triggers the executory contract provisions, and the debtor (whether franchisee or franchisor) therefore is permitted to assume or reject the contract in the course of the proceedings.

Franchising, though, also is governed by state law, and this adds a layer of complexity to the contractual analysis. If the *franchisee* files a bankruptcy petition, the protections of any applicable state law governing termination of franchise interests will determine the ability of the franchisor to terminate the agreement.[12] If the franchise agreement has not been terminated under its own terms or in accordance with the provisions of state law prior to the filing of the petition in bankruptcy, the franchise agreement and all rights associated with it become property of the estate and the franchisor is enjoined from direct termination. Franchise laws may provide for rights of termination upon non-performance by the franchisee, including the failure to comply with operational standards and requirements or financial payment obligations. While these rights might give rise to a franchisor's right to terminate the agreement in the absence of bankruptcy, if termination is not completed before the filing of the petition there would normally be no right of automatic termination in bankruptcy. An important distinction may exist, though, between steps needed to effectuate termination and the running of a statutory or contractual notice period. In this case, if the franchisor has taken every step necessary to terminate the agreement and all that remains is the conclusion of a notice period, courts have held that a bankruptcy petition does not terminate the notice and therefore the franchise agreement can be deemed to have terminated before the filing.[13]

What can the franchisor do in a case in which the agreement has not been terminated prior to bankruptcy? Given that the franchise agreement becomes property of the estate, the franchisor can move to lift the stay with respect to the franchisee's rights under the agreement. Here, any showing that the franchisor would be entitled to terminate the agreement in the absence of bankruptcy likely would be sufficient to lift the stay, but other facts may condition the court's ruling on the question. In any case, whether involving a right to terminate outside of bankruptcy or not, the franchisor must satisfy all of the requirements of the Code pertaining to lifting the automatic stay, as would any other claimant seeking access to property of the estate.

Thus far we have implicitly assumed that the debtor/franchisee might wish to continue the franchise agreement and therefore is attempting to secure the protection of the Code and state law in order to defend against the franchisor's attempted termination. Conversely, the franchisee has the right to reject the franchise agreement, just as any other contract. While a franchisor seeking to terminate might be willing to accept this outcome, note that there is nothing in the Code that compels the debtor to reject expeditiously in a Chapter 11 proceeding, other than the time limits applicable to proposing and confirming a plan. A franchisor unwilling to wait may either seek relief from the stay or petition for the imposition of a time limit on assumption or rejection.[14] Remember, too, that upon rejection the contracting party has an unsecured claim against the estate for breach of contract; in a franchise case, this may or may not be relevant to the franchisor if the rejection accomplishes a desired termination. The value of the claim, in other words, will depend upon the facts and the amount owed under the contract and able to be collected from the debtor/franchisee.

Another option we have not previously discussed is the assumption and assignment of a franchise agreement. If the debtor assumes the franchise agreement as an executory contract, recall that all existing defaults must be cured. Having done so, the debtor may assign the agreement to another party. In a franchise agreement case, though, the debtor/franchisee may not be able to assign the agreement if valid contractual restrictions exist. In particular, assignment can be prevented where the agreement limits transfer or assignment of trademarks, often one of the main benefits of the franchise relationship.[15] This provides protection of the franchisor's intellectual property rights, as well as the right to choose its representatives.

Thus far, we have looked only at franchisee bankruptcy. Obviously, as with GM in the auto dealership context, it is not only franchisees that encounter financial difficulty and eventually file a bankruptcy petition. In most such cases, the franchisor has an interest in maintaining its franchise network, and consequently assumption of existing franchise agreements probably will be the norm. With respect to those franchisees that the franchisor might wish to terminate, the franchisor may be able to time the termination and bankruptcy petition such that termination is accomplished entirely pre-petition, thereby avoiding some of the complications mentioned earlier. In cases where termination would not be permissible outside of bankruptcy, the Code once again would not give rise to a right of rejection. The franchisee's rights would be protected by applicable state law, but if state law does not give rise to such rights, then the Code's treatment of executory contracts would prevail.

A final consideration applicable primarily to franchisee bankruptcies concerns the small business debtor provisions inserted into the Code by BAPCPA. Particularly if the franchisee owns only a single franchise, as compared with the case of one who has an interest in multiple locations, it is very likely that the franchisee will qualify as a small business as defined by BAPCPA. Given the condensed time limits and increased reporting mandated under the new provisions, this may be beneficial to franchisors dealing with bankrupt franchisees. Again, this is an area that may be the topic of conversation as developments progress under the new law.

5.4 Selling Claims and Interests

One of the more recent developments in bankruptcy practice is the increasing availability of markets for the sale of bankruptcy claims and interests. Many claimants, recognizing the limitations on their claims or simply the amount of time necessary to complete the bankruptcy, may wish to reduce their claims to readily available cash, even if doing so means settling for much less than might be forthcoming upon plan confirmation (or even in liquidation). Buyers approach these deals with two primary goals: (1) Achieving a relatively quick profit on a claim acquired for less than market value; or (2) acquiring a sufficient number of claims to effectively gain control of the bankruptcy proceedings and perhaps the debtor itself. The latter strategy may permit an otherwise viable debtor to be acquired for far less than even liquidation value, on the expectation that post-bankruptcy value will be significant and ongoing or that assets can be stripped and sold for far more than the pro rata cost of the underlying claims.

Apart from the near certainty of a discount from actual claim value, there are several other common features associated with claims transactions. Buyers are assuming the risk that the claim actually will be collectible for more than the discounted price. In other words, buyers are exposed to unforeseen or unknowable facts, and given this they will almost always seek contractual protection against more commonly encountered contingencies. Among these are challenges to the validity of the claim, which may entail significant cost to defend even if ultimately defeated. A common approach of buyers is to require a right to sell the claim back to the seller upon a challenge based on validity, preference, rightful title, or some other legitimate argument. At the very least, buyers may require the seller to assume the burden of defending such challenges.

Sellers also should be aware that, if they hold a seat on a creditors' committee, they may be subject to the equivalent of an insider trading charge based on greater access to information concerning the debtor than is available to other creditors. Serving as a creditor representative on a committee carries with it a fiduciary duty to fairly represent the class. One can see, then, how such an obligation might give rise to questions about, and ultimately liability for, a claimant's sale of its claim while serving in this capacity.

In sum, a claim sale is not a panacea for the anxious claimant. Each proposed transaction will need to be evaluated carefully, with an eye not only to the economics involved but also the contingencies and limitations imposed by the buyers or under law. But a sale does enable the claimant to liquidate its position more quickly than waiting for the conclusion of the case, and therefore may be a valid option for some claimants. From the buyer's perspective, claims purchases afford the opportunity for return on investment capital and/or control of the debtor entity.

5.5 Governance Issues

Corporate governance as a principle is concerned with the process by which decisions affecting the organization are made and accountability is maintained for the benefit of the shareholders. One of the concerns arising from the operation of the modern corporation is the existence of information asymmetries between insiders and outsiders, potentially even including the board. Given the alterations in practice created by bankruptcy, there is a credible argument to be made that the Code exacerbates these information asymmetries due to the possibility of substituting bankruptcy reports for those normally required by the securities laws.

We will begin our discussion by observing that bankruptcy does not relieve the debtor of its responsibility to comply with SEC rules and regulations pertaining to the reporting process. But a company in bankruptcy might alter its reporting obligations by requesting what is known as modified reporting, which allows the debtor to use its Chapter 11 filings, especially including its disclosure statement, in lieu of separate reports required by the SEC under normal circumstances. The SEC retains the right to approve such requests, and usually will not accede to a request in the absence of compelling circumstances that indicate compliance with routine reporting requirements is infeasible or overly burdensome. That leaves the debtor with the election to deregister altogether, which does suspend reporting requirements. However, there are limitations on the availability of this election.[16]

Another consideration relevant to the issue of disclosure concerns the application of the Sarbanes–Oxley Act, the law passed in the wake of the Enron scandal to mandate changes in financial records and reporting obligations. One of the key provisions of Sarbanes–Oxley Act was its certification requirement, under which the CEO must certify and attest to the accuracy of all financial accounts and representations. Two issues may arise in connection with Sarbanes–Oxley Act's compliance in bankruptcy. First, the certification process normally gives rights to shareholders, but in bankruptcy shareholder interests are subordinated to those of creditors and other claimants. We have discussed the potential shift in fiduciary duties from shareholders to creditors in financially distressed firms, which, if recognized by a given jurisdiction, clearly would extend Sarbanes–Oxley Act's certification in favor of claimants in a bankruptcy. Even without formal recognition of this doctrine, claimants are likely to make the case that they are entitled to rely on such certifications and that any breach gives them an additional claim in the bankruptcy proceedings.

In turn, this raises the second issue, which is whether the bankruptcy and subsequently discovered financial distress can be used as conclusive evidence that Sarbanes–Oxley Act's certifications were inaccurate, misleading, or even fraudulent. To date, there has been no clear answer to this question. But Sarbanes–Oxley Act seems to have resulted in the potential to assert additional claims in bankruptcy either against the debtor itself or against individual officers and directors.

A final governance-related issue concerns voting rights and the selection of company officers and directors. With respect to this issue, bankruptcy marks a significant departure from pre-petition practice given the *de facto* disfranchisement of the debtor's shareholders. We pointed to the Code's treatment of officer and director identification as we discussed the development of the plan. It is worth emphasizing here that existing shareholders commonly do not vote on the plan, often because their interests are completely eliminated. This being the case, it is left to other claimants, while negotiating the content of the plan, to propose nominees or oppose those of the debtor, which may result in holding up plan confirmation as a result. Thus, officers and directors are another negotiating point, but between claimants and the debtor, not the shareholders.

5.6 Derivatives in Bankruptcy

As we know from the experience of the past few years and the steady stream of news headlines, derivatives are highly complex and subject to more risk than some practitioners and proponents once had assumed. We will not engage in an extensive discussion of derivatives here, but we will attempt to provide a broad-brush description of what derivatives are and how their use is treated, and the issues they raise, in bankruptcy.

At a basic level, derivatives are contracts that represent bets made by the contracting parties on the price or some other attribute of an underlying object. Insurance policies are, in effect, derivatives, as are futures contracts and options. These are basic forms of the concept, which can extend to highly complex and sophisticated arrangements such as credit default swaps, interest rate swaps, collateralized debt obligations, and the like. Moreover, it is not even necessary to own an interest in the object of the derivatives contract; one simply may take a position on the future value or the occurrence of some event. For example, you and I are free to enter into an agreement based on whether or not a particular nation defaults on its sovereign debt. Indeed, it is this latter feature that has caused concern in light of recent financial mayhem, because without ownership or direct interest as a prerequisite there is no limitation on the number of potential contracts, and hence liability, that can exist at a given point in time.

The use of derivatives presents several issues in bankruptcy. One concerns the relationship between the contracting parties, commonly known as counterparties. In common derivatives practice of the past, a contract between two counterparties might call for collateralization of the payment obligations of one or both. When one party then filed for bankruptcy, there were some questions concerning the precise nature of the interests in that property held by the non-bankrupt counterparty: Was it ownership or a security interest? The problem was magnified if the property actually was physically transferred. Under a series of amendments to the Code, most recently in the BAPCPA, derivatives contracts are given substantial leeway. If one reviews the automatic stay provisions reproduced in Chapter 2 and the associated hypotheticals, one will note language in the exceptions covering one form of a derivative arrangement (others, not quoted, also are included within the provision for exceptions to the automatic stay). Thus, upon the bankruptcy of one counterparty, the other may be able to avoid the stay and execute upon its interest in collateral (depending upon the specifics of the arrangement and its coverage by the actual language of the exception). At this writing, it is not yet clear how the Dodd-Frank Act's requirements for settlement and clearing of derivatives contracts will affect or change bankruptcy practice, but it is not unreasonable to assume that by somewhat rationalizing the settlement process the Act, together with the BAPCPA and earlier amendments, will result in smoother assertions of interest. As usual, though, only time will tell.

Astute readers may question whether, even if acceptable as it concerns the stay, recovery of collateral might nevertheless be subject to avoidance as a fraudulent transfer. The answer, technically, is yes if the basic elements are satisfied. In other words, just because we are dealing with a derivative and a permitted execution on collateral in satisfaction of an obligation, we are not immune to other prohibitions of the Code. But recognizing the potential application of fraudulent transfer doctrine, the drafters of the BAPCPA responded once more, exempting such actions from the coverage of the Code's provisions on fraudulent transfers. Only those activities involving actual fraud, or which for some reason are contractually subject to avoidance, may be treated as fraudulent transfers.

As might be expected, there is a significant amount of debate and controversy surrounding these provisions, including questions as to both policy and practice.[17] For example, the amendments make no distinctions between and among different types of derivative arrangements, such as hedging contracts on the one hand and speculative contracts on the other. Surely the nature of the contract involved, and the exposure created thereby, should have some bearing upon its treatment in bankruptcy. Speculative derivatives, for example, would seem well suited to remain subject to fraudulent transfer attack. At present there seems to be little or no movement in this direction.

Apart from questions involving rights to property, though, is the nature of the claim itself and the incentives that might be created thereby. In other words, if we are dealing with an uncollateralized derivatives contract, or perhaps a residual claim following execution on the collateral, what happens to that claim in bankruptcy and how will the counterparty holding the claim proceed? There seems to be little doubt that the counterparty would be entitled to assert its claim, and be recognized, in a bankruptcy proceeding under a contract. But here is where the matter gets interesting: Suppose that the counterparty's position was that the debtor *would* be insolvent or have a value below a certain level, which, if true, would result in payoff under the contract. This is, in essence, the nature of a credit default swap, in which an insurer (say, AIG) would be obligated to pay if the triggering event occurred. In such a case, the payoff on the credit default swap might net a higher return than the counterparty's claim on the underlying obligation of the debtor. What would be its incentives in bankruptcy then? Believe it or not, such a creditor would be better off arguing that the debtor's property and assets were worth too much! Indeed, we have already witnessed such behavior.[18]

In sum, derivatives generally are accorded protections not available to other contractual relationships. In this sense, they do not pose a direct problem in bankruptcy, other than the possible dissipation of assets otherwise reachable by traditional claimants. This represents a policy concern, if not a practical one. More practical concerns arise when we consider potential incentives resulting from a claimant's position in a derivative. Claimants holding derivatives interests may skew the reorganization of an otherwise viable business, complicating or even scuttling the process. Much more could, of course, be said about the topic of derivatives, more than can be dealt with here. For now, remember the issues of preferential disposition of derivative claims and the potential for perverse incentives.

Notes

Chapter 1

1. It is important to note that bankruptcy, like many legal concepts, varies by jurisdiction. There are many different bankruptcy regimes throughout the world, and the American approach to reorganization is fairly unique in its procedures and its generally forgiving stance toward debtor organizations. Whether this is good or bad is a matter for a different forum; for the purposes of this book, the reader should simply be aware that the frame of reference is American law and that resolution of the issues discussed here can, and probably will, be different in other countries.
2. References to Chapters 7 and 11 of the Code always mean, respectively, liquidation and reorganization. These are the two principal bankruptcy methodologies under the Code for debtor corporations. I attempt to distinguish references to text chapters by reference to the text, but for simplicity, remember that, since there are only five chapters in this book, a reference to Chapter 7 or Chapter 11 means the Code's liquidation or reorganization provisions.
3. Hawkins (2010); Stempel (2010).
4. Keehner and Helyar (2010).
5. Campoy and Futterman (2010); Sorkin (2010).
6. Keehner and Helyar (2010).
7. Church (2010).
8. Campoy and Futterman (2010).
9. Brown (2010).
10. Campoy and Futterman (2010).
11. Brown (2010); Keehner and Helyar (2010).
12. See text Chapter 5 for more on prepackaged bankruptcies.
13. *Credit Lyonnais Bank Nederland, N.V. v. Pathe Communications Corp.*, 1991 WL 277613 (Del.Ch. Dec. 30, 1991). LoPucki and Whitford (1993a) also provide evidence that managerial alignment with either creditors or shareholders is a function of firm solvency.
14. See, for example, Hambrick and D'Aveni (1988, 1992), highlighting the "downward spiral" phenomenon.
15. Blackstone (1765–1769). See also Tabb (1991) for a summary and discussion of many of the historical developments following in this section. The reference here to a broken counter or bench also apparently reflects the

ancient practice of breaking a debtor tradesman's workbench, thereby rendering him commercially bankrupt.

16. Johns (1987).
17. Madison (1961/1788).
18. Skeel (2001).
19. Tabb (1991).
20. Note here the precursor to today's debates, and arguably the foundational premises of the Bankruptcy Abuse Prevention and Consumer Protection Act of 2005 (BAPCPA).
21. Skeel (2001).
22. Tabb (1991).
23. Skeel (2001).
24. Warren (2008).
25. Critically, the 2005 BAPCPA in effect reinstates the dichotomy in the case of small business bankruptcies, as will be discussed later in this text. See Chapter 5 below.
26. Individuals still file separately, under Chapter 13, or may liquidate under Chapter 7.
27. See Chapter 4 of the text, below, for further elaboration of these concepts.
28. LoPucki and Whitford (1991); LoPucki (2005).
29. Interested readers may wish to review, among many other reputable sources, CCH's briefing on the BAPCPA, accessible at http://www.cch.com/bankrutpcy/bankruptcy_04-21.pdf.
30. Again, see text Chapter 5 below for more on small business bankruptcies.
31. Warren (2008).
32. LoPucki (1990).

Chapter 2

1. Bankruptcy Code, 11 U.S.C. Section 301(a). Throughout the text, subsequent citations to the Code will refer only to the specific section, unless a different title is at issue.
2. Section 101 (41).
3. Section 109(a), (b), and (d).
4. Note that, technically, under the definition of "person," and given the fact that other exclusions from that definition are specified by the Code while individuals are not, an individual may file under Chapter 11. This allows coverage of the Chapter 11 process for small businesses that are operated as unincorporated sole proprietorships.
5. Section 706, governing conversions of Chapter 7 cases to Chapter 11, and Section 1112, governing conversions of Chapter 11 cases to Chapter 7.

6. 28 U.S.C. Section 1408.

7. LoPucki (2005).

8. LoPucki (1993b); LoPucki and Whitford (1990).

9. LoPucki (2005).

10. 28 U.S.C. Section 1412.

11. See Alderman (2006) for some general suggestions.

12. See, for example, Lawless, Ferris, Jayaraman, and Makhija (1994); Lawless and Ferris (1997); Ferris and Lawless (2000).

13. Bermant and Flynn (1998).

14. Warren and Westbrook (2009).

15. Hambrick and D'Aveni (1988, 1992).

16. See, for example, Sutton and Callahan (1987).

17. Adler (1996).

18. Kahneman and Tversky (1979).

19. Sanders (2001); Sanders and Carpenter (2003); Sanders and Hambrick (2007); Wiseman and Gomez-Mejia (1998).

20. Donoher (2004).

21. *Credit Lyonnais Bank Nederland, N.V. v. Pathe Communications Corp.*, 1991 WL 277613 (Del.Ch. Dec. 30, 1991).

22. See, for example, LoPucki and Whitford (1993a, 1993b); Weiss (1990). The distinction between this outcome and the Donoher (2004) study lies in the latter's focus on managerial ownership, which seems to delay filing. Equity broadly held may promote the outcomes suggested here.

23. Warren and Westbrook (2009), and note 14 above.

24. Section 109.

25. *In re SGL Carbon Corp.*, 200 F.3d 154 (3rd Cir. 1999).

26. See Rule 1007, Federal Rules of Bankruptcy Procedure. Hereinafter, all rules cited refer to this source and will be referred to simply by rule number.

27. 28 U.S.C. Section 586.

28. Section 341; see also Rule 2003.

29. Section 362.

30. Section 362(d); see also Blum (2006) at 260.

31. Section 362(d)(1).

32. Section 362(d)(2). Two other provisions of the statute apply only to cases involving real property or a single-asset real property debtor.

33. Section 362(g).

34. Section 361.

35. Section 362(d)(2).

36. Section 303(g).

37. Section 303(f).

38. Section 303(h).

Chapter 3

1. Section 541(a).
2. Section 541(a)(1).
3. Section 541(a)(2)(A).
4. Section 541(b)(1).
5. Section 541(b)(2).
6. Section 541(c)(1).
7. *In re Platt*, 292 B.R. 12 (Bankr. D. Mass. 2003).
8. Section 541(a).
9. Section 542.
10. Section 541(a)(6) and (7).
11. Section 552(a).
12. Section 554.
13. Rule 3002.
14. Rule 3003.
15. Section 510.
16. Section 510.
17. Warren (2008).
18. Section 506(b).
19. Complicating factors associated with interest accrual, such as the permissibility of a stipulated default rate, are beyond the scope of this work. In most cases, use of the lower base contract rate is the safer course of action based on existing case law.
20. Section 506(a)(1).
21. Section 507(b).
22. Section 364.
23. Section 364(d).
24. Section 363(c)(1).
25. Section 363(c)(2).
26. Section 363(d).
27. Section 363(f).
28. Section 544(a).
29. Section 544(b).
30. See also Chapter 5, below.
31. Section 547(b)
32. Section 101(54).
33. Section 547(c).
34. Section 547(a)(2).
35. Section 547(c)(2).
36. Section 547(c)(3).

37. Section 547(c)(4).
38. Section 547(c)(5).
39. Section 548.
40. A permutation of the available window of opportunity for avoidance is considered below in Chapter 5.
41. Section 548(a)(1)(B).
42. *BFP v. Resolution Trust Corp.*, 511 U.S. 531 (1994).
43. Section 548(c).
44. Section 549.
45. Section 363; see text section 3.3.1.
46. Section 363(e).

Chapter 4

1. Recall that Section 706 permits various interested parties to seek conversion.
2. Section 702(a).
3. Section 704.
4. Section 705.
5. Section 721.
6. Section 542; see text section 3.1.1.
7. As per Section 364; also see text section 3.2.5.3. Be aware that the court also may permit the other forms of post-petition financing delineated in the Code and above, including conferral of administrative priorities or superpriorities under Section 364.
8. Section 721.
9. Section 724.
10. Section 510; see also text section 3.2.4.
11. Section 724(a).
12. Section 724(b).
13. Section 725.
14. Section 725.
15. Section 726.
16. Section 726(a)(5).
17. See text section 3.2.5.1.
18. Section 726(b).
19. Section 727(a)(1).
20. Section 1107. This would exclude the obligation to investigate the debtor. Section 1104 permits the court to appoint an examiner in cases in which the need to investigate arises.
21. Section 1104.

22. Warren (2008).
23. Sections 1102 and 1103.
24. See Blum (2006) at 400. The term is not defined in the Code, and instead is based upon legal commentary favorably cited in the legislative history of Section 365, the executory contract provision of the Code.
25. Section 365. In a Chapter 7 case, the decision to assume or reject must be made within 60 days of the filing of the petition. Additionally, other parties to the Chapter 11 proceeding may petition the court to order assumption or rejection within a definite time period.
26. Blum (2006).
27. There are also special provisions applicable to the treatment of loan commitments, intellectual property, shopping center leases, and other kinds of specific real and personal property.
28. The same result holds in the case of a non-executory contract, as where I pay the contractor up front. I have a general unsecured claim dating from the date prior to the bankruptcy petition.
29. Section 507(a)(1); also see text section 3.2.5 above.
30. Section 365(g)(1).
31. Section 1113 was enacted in 1984.
32. Section 1113(b)(1).
33. Section 1113(c).
34. Section 1114(c).
35. Section 1114(g).
36. Section 1122.
37. If nothing else, courts are likely to intervene in cases in which it is apparent that the only reason for the proposed classification is to create a favorable outcome.
38. Section 1121(b).
39. Section 1121(d)(2)(B).
40. Section 1123.
41. Section 1124.
42. Section 1123(b).
43. Section 1125.
44. The provision for adequate information explicitly reserves a highly subjective right of interpretation and judgment in favor of the court, which is entitled to consider the complexity of the case and the cost and benefit inherent in any additional required disclosures. See Section 1125(a)(1).
45. See Chapter 5 for more on this topic.
46. Section 1129.
47. LoPucki and Whitford (1993a, 1993b); Weiss (1990).
48. Section 1124(2).

49. Section 1126.
50. Section 1129.
51. Section 1129(b)(1).
52. Readers may recall the discussion, in Chapter 3, of undersecured creditors, those whose collateral is not of sufficient value to support the creditor's claim in full. Section 1111 provides these creditors with an alternate mechanism to determine fair and equitable treatment. This is one of the most abstruse provisions in the entire Code and thus will not be considered in this book (indeed, some view the provision as so immune to interpretation that its meaning is inferred only by adherence to historical standard practice). It is sufficient for our purposes to note that an undersecured creditor may elect to have its claim handled under Section 1111, which essentially allows the unsecured portion of the creditor's claim to be eliminated and for the entire claim to be treated as secured. The threat of this option may be sufficient to provide the creditor with more negotiating leverage than would exist without it.
53. Section 1141.

Chapter 5

1. Section 101(51D). The amount is subject to periodic adjustment. The current figure was last adjusted as of April 1, 2007.
2 Rule 1020
3. Section 1116.
4. Section 1121(e).
5. Section 101(51D)(A).
6. Section 1121(a).
7. Section 1126(b).
8. Section 544(b). The precise window will depend on state law, and in particular on the state's adoption and amendment, if any, of the Uniform Fraudulent Transfers Act.
9. Section 548; see also text section 3.3.2.
10. Alesci, Weiss, and Banerjee (2012).
11. Blair and Lafontaine (2005).
12. State laws may govern conventional franchises or dealerships. One of the issues presented by the GM bankruptcy concerned the company's ability to terminate dealerships. Most states have statutes that govern dealership arrangements that provide a number of formal protections not necessarily available to the traditional franchisee.
13. See, for example, *In re Diversified Washes of Vandalia, Inc.*, 147 B.R. 23 (Bankr. S.D. Ohio 1992).

14. Section 365(d)(2).
15. See, for example, *Wellington Vision, Inc. v. Pearle Vision, Inc.,* 364 B.R. 129 (S.D. Fla. 2007).
16. Full treatment of these securities law issues is beyond the scope of this book. Those seeking more specific information are encouraged to consult the Securities Exchange Act of 1934 and the associated regulations issued by the SEC.
17. Coy (2009).
18. *The Economist* (2009).

References

Adler, B. E. (1996). Bankruptcy and risk allocation. In J. S. Bhandari, & L. A. Weiss (Eds.), *Corporate bankruptcy: Economic and legal perspectives* (pp. 190–206). New York: Cambridge University Press.

Alderman, M. H. (2006). *Chapter 11 business reorganizations for business leaders, accountants and lawyers.* Denver, CO: Outskirts Press.

Alesci, C., Weiss, M., & Banerjee, Devin. (2012, March 19). Payday. *Bloomberg Businessweek*, 57–58.

Bermant, G., & Flynn, E.D. (1998). Bankruptcy by the numbers. *American Bankruptcy Institute Journal XVII*, 8–13.

Blackstone, W. (1765–1769). *Commentaries on the laws of England.* Oxford: Clarendon Press.

Blair, R. D., & Lafontaine, F. (2005). *The economics of franchising.* New York: Cambridge University Press.

Blum, B. A. (2006). *Bankruptcy and debtor/creditor* (IVth ed.). New York: Aspen Press.

Brown, A. K. (2010, August 5). Nolan Ryan group wins auction for Rangers. *Associated Press.*

Campoy, A., & Futterman, M. (2010, August 5). Nolan Ryan group wins Texas Rangers. *The Wall Street Journal.*

Church, S. (2010, July 19). JP Morgan sues Texas Rangers for changing stadium lease before bankruptcy. *Bloomberg.*

Coy, P. (2009, May 25). When even failure stops working. *BusinessWeek*, 16–17.

Donoher, W. J. (2004). To file or not to file? Systemic incentives, corporate control, and the bankruptcy decision. *Journal of Management 30*, 239–262.

The Economist. (2009, June 20). No empty threat. p. 79.

Ferris, S. P., & Lawless, R. M. (2000). The expenses of financial distress: The direct costs of Chapter 11. *University of Pittsburgh Law Review 61*, 629–669.

Hambrick, D. C., & D'Aveni, R. A. (1988). Large corporate failures as downward spirals. *Administrative Science Quarterly 33*, 1–23.

Hambrick, D. C., & D'Aveni, R. A. (1992). Top team deterioration as part of the downward spiral of large corporate bankruptcies. *Management Science 38*, 1445–1466.

Hawkins, S. (2010, May 24). Texas Rangers bankruptcy: Team to be sold by midsummer. *Huffington Post.*

Johns, C. H. W. (1987). *Babylonian and assyrian laws, contracts and letters.* New York: Legal Classics Library, Gryphon Editions.

Kahneman, D., & Tversky, A. (1979). Prospect theory: An analysis of decision under risk. *Econometrica 47*, 263–291.

Keehner, J., & Helyar, J. (2010, May 25). Texas Rangers baseball team files for bankruptcy. *Bloomberg*.

Lawless, R. M., & Ferris, S. P. (1997). Professional fees and other direct costs in Chapter 7 business liquidations. *Washington University Law Quarterly 75*, 1207–1236.

Lawless, R. M., Ferris, S. P., Jayaraman, N., & Makhija, A. K. (1994). A glimpse at professional fees and other direct costs in small-firm bankruptcies. *University of Illinois Law Review 1994*, 847–879.

LoPucki, L. M. (1993). The trouble with Chapter 11. *University of Wisconsin Law Review 1993*, 729–760.

LoPucki, L. M. (2005). *Courting failure*. Ann Arbor, MI: University of Michigan Press.

LoPucki, L. M., & Whitford, W. C. (1990). Bargaining over equity's share in the bankruptcy reorganization of large, publicly held companies. *University of Pennsylvania Law Review 139*, 125–196.

LoPucki, L. M., & Whitford, W. C. (1991). Venue choice and forum shopping in the bankruptcy reorganization of large, publicly held companies. *University of Wisconsin Law Review 1991*, 11–63.

LoPucki, L. M., & Whitford, W. C. (1993a). Corporate governance in the bankruptcy reorganization of large, publicly held companies. *University of Pennsylvania Law Review 141*, 669–800.

LoPucki, L. M., & Whitford, W. C. (1993b). Patterns in the bankruptcy reorganization of large, publicly held companies. *Cornell Law Review 78*, 597–618.

Madison, J. (1961/1788). Federalist No. 42. *The federalist papers*. New York: New American Library.

Sanders, Wm. G., & Hambrick, D. C. (2007). Swinging for the fences: The effects of CEO stock options on company risk taking and performance. *Academy of Management Journal 50*(5), 1053–1078.

Sanders, Wm. G. (2001). Behavioral responses of CEOs to stock ownership and stock option pay. *Academy of Management Journal 44*, 477–492.

Sanders, Wm. G., & Carpenter, M. A. (2003). Strategic satisficing? A behavioral-agency theory perspective on stock repurchase program announcements. *Academy of Management Journal 46*, 160–178.

Skeel, D. A., Jr. (2001). *Debt's dominion*. Princeton, NJ: Princeton University Press.

Sorkin, A. R. (Ed.). (2010, May 24). Texas Rangers enter bankruptcy to expedite sale. *The New York Times DealBook*.

Stempel, J. (2010, May 24). Texas Rangers file bankruptcy. *Reuters*.

Sutton, R. I., & Callahan, A. L. (1987). The stigma of bankruptcy: Spoiled organizational image and its management. *Academy of Management Journal 30*, 405–436.

Tabb, C. J. (1991). The historical evolution of the bankruptcy discharge. *American Bankruptcy Law Journal 65*, 325–371.

Warren, E. (2008). *Chapter 11: Reorganizing American business.* New York: Aspen Publishers.

Warren, E., & Westbrook, J. (2009). The success of Chapter 11: A challenge to the critics. *University of Michigan Law Review 107*, 603–642.

Weiss, L. A. (1990). Bankruptcy resolution: Direct costs and violation of priority of claims. *Journal of Financial Economics 27*, 285–314.

Wiseman, R. M., & Gomez-Mejia, L. R. (1998). A behavioral agency model of managerial risk taking. *Academy of Management Review 23*, 133–153.

Index

Announcing the Business Expert Press Digital Library

Concise E-books Business Students Need for Classroom and Research

This book can also be purchased in an e-book collection by your library as

- a one-time purchase,
- that is owned forever,
- allows for simultaneous readers,
- has no restrictions on printing, and
- can be downloaded as PDFs from within the library community.

Our digital library collections are a great solution to beat the rising cost of textbooks. e-books can be loaded into their course management systems or onto student's e-book readers.

The **Business Expert Press** digital libraries are very affordable, with no obligation to buy in future years. For more information, please visit **www.businessexpertpress.com/librarians**. To set up a trial in the United States, please contact **Adam Chesler** at *adam.chesler@businessexpertpress. com* for all other regions, contact **Nicole Lee** at *nicole.lee@igroupnet.com*.

OTHER TITLES IN OUR STRATEGIC MANAGEMENT COLLECTION

Collection Editor: **William Q. Judge, Old Dominion University**

- *An Executive's Primer on the Strategy of Social Networks* by Mason Carpenter
- *Building Strategy and Performance Through Time: The Critical Path* by Kim Warren
- *Knowledge Management: Begging for a Bigger Role 2e* by Arnold Kransdorff
- *Sustainable Business: An Executive's Primer* by Nancy Landrum and Sally Edwards
- *Mergers and Acquisitions: Turmoil in Top Management Teams* by Jeffrey Krug
- *Positive Management: Increasing Employee Productivity* by Jack Walters
- *Business Goes Virtual: Realizing the Value of Collaboration, Social and Virtual Strategies* by John Girard and JoAnn Girard
- *Fundamentals of Global Strategy: A Business Model Approach* by Cornelis de Kluyver
- *A Leader's Guide to Virtual Business* by John Girard and JoAnn Girard
- *Grow by Focusing on What Matters: Competitive Strategy in 3-Circles* by Joe Urbany and Jim Davis
- *The Strategic Management of Higher Education Institutions: Serving Students as Customers for Institutional Growth* by Hamid Kazeroony
- *A Stakeholder's Approach to Issues Management* by Robert Boutilier
- *Achieving Excellence in Management: Identifying and Learning from Bad Practices* by Andrew Kilner

www.ingramcontent.com/pod-product-compliance
Lightning Source LLC
Chambersburg PA
CBHW071858200326

41519CB00016B/4442